WORKSHOPS WORK!

a parent's guide to facilitating
writer's workshops
for kids

WORKSHOPS WORK!

a parent's guide to facilitating
writer's workshops
for kids

by Patricia Zaballos

Happy workshopping!
patricia zaballos

For ordering information and additional resources, visit
www.patriciazaballos.com

Printed in the United States of America

This is for all the kids who have workshopped with me over the years. Thank you for allowing me into your wondrous writing worlds.

CONTENTS

Part One: The Workshop

Part Two: The Toolbox

part one:

THE WORKSHOP

1.
WRITER'S WORKSHOPS:
AN INTRODUCTION

"My son *hates* writing."

The mother almost whispers these words to me. Her statement is part confession, part apology. She knows I work with kid-writers; she knows that I love writing. In four wistful words she manages to convey her own sense of failure and a load of lost hope. She thinks she's alone.

I wish I knew how many times I've had a parent confess a version of those four words to me. If I had book for every one, you'd beg to visit my library. Yet each of these parents seems to think that their situation is atypical. Classrooms of kids write hour after hour, day after day, but *their* kid doesn't want to.

So I tell them: Lots of kids dislike writing. *Lots* of kids. Maybe even most kids, at some point in their childhoods. At one time my oldest was a writing-hater too.

And then I ask: *Why* does your child dislike writing? Is it the physical task of writing, and the spelling, the grammar, the punctuation that the child dreads? If the physical writing is a hurdle for the child, then I recommend parents explore taking dictation from him or her. You can read a brief introduction to dictation in Part Two of this guide.

Or is the child's dislike of writing based in something else? Lots of kids, it seems, simply don't see the point of writing. Why go to all that trouble just to put your words on a page or screen? Which leads me to this question for parents: does your child have an audience for his or her writing? Does your daughter have someone she's writing *for*? Does your son have a reason to write—beyond the fact that Mom or Dad thinks it's a good idea?

Many parents are so anxious to get their kids writing that they forget why we write. If we aren't writing for a school or work assignment, *we write because we have something we want to share with someone.* Sure, some of us write for ourselves: in journals, on cardboard coasters, to work something out, to remember, for the pleasure of playing with words. But most of us, most of the time, write to communicate with others.

If we want kids to write, we don't need to find them paper with perfectly spaced lines. We don't need to search out penmanship worksheets or curricula with appealing writing prompts. What we need to find for our kids is an audience. We need to give kids a *reason* to write, so the desire to write can begin to bubble— and an audience is often what it takes.

One of the easiest ways I know to conjure an audience is to start a writer's workshop.

Conjure is an apt word here because, in my experience, writer's workshops are almost magical in their ability to motivate kids' writing. I've facilitated a variety of groups in my home for over a dozen years, working with kids as young as four and as old as seventeen. Before that, I taught elementary school, and devoted a portion of each day to a writer's workshop in my classroom. After all these years, I'm still surprised at how a workshop can inspire a child's desire to write. I see it in the kids from my current group, overheard at the park, asking each other, "What are you reading at the workshop tomorrow?" I see it in the ten-year-old who emails, begging me to hold our bi-monthly workshops every week, "Please!!!!!!!!!" I saw it a few years back in the teenage boy who cranked out regular installments of a *Twilight* series spoof, because the other workshop kids cheered and whined for them. In the kids who arrive at my house on workshop day, and scurry off to a corner to scratch out the unfinished ending to a story—because they don't want to miss the party. In my own son, my oldest, who hollered about how much he hated writing at seven, but months later, after we'd started our first workshop, could be found at the kitchen table, scribbling away at his own *Captain Underpants* comics before he'd even finished his morning glass of orange juice.

A writer's workshop may not have such an effect on every child, but I'll make the audacious claim that it will have such an effect on most kids. It's a powerful motivator, and it's hard not to use magic as its metaphor. I'm not the only one to think so; I've heard facilitators of other workshops and writing clubs for kids make similar claims.

I like the writer's workshop because it's fun to share my stories and hear other stories. It helps motivate me to write more. —Cecilia, 10

The workshop has given me a fun and enjoyable reason to write whatever I like, and however I like. —Robin, 13

Being in the writers' workshop was a turning point for me. I began to see writing as fun, and not just work. I had never seen myself as a writer before, but in the group I had fun and recognized my potential. Feedback from the group gave me confidence. I learned to get my ideas on the page without second-guessing myself. Now that I'm in my first year of high school (and very first year of school), I see that the writers' workshop helped me develop my critical thinking skills in preparation for high school. I feel better prepared for the writing assignments I have at school. —Nathan, former participant and current high school student

I loved the writers workshop because it gave me an amazing outlet to express my creative impulses. Having an environment of open peers willing to hear my thoughts, stories, and ideas was always a powerful inspiration to keep me thinking and dreaming. —Henry, former participant and current college student

Yet, for all it offers, a workshop is a fairly simple gathering to facilitate. We're talking big payoff with minimal effort. Really, all you need to provide is a place for kids to share their writing, and a little help in cultivating a nurturing atmosphere. This guide will show you how to do that. Whether you're a home-schooling parent trying to make writing more meaningful for your child, or the parent of a schooled child seeking a less standards-based, more creative writing experience for him or her, a writer's workshop may be just what you're looking for.

What, exactly, is a writer's workshop?

A workshop is simply a gathering where writers share their writing and offer one another feedback. Some groups have writers bring work from home; some do the writing during the workshop; some use a combination of both.

Historically, the workshop model of writing instruction began at the University of Iowa in the 1930s, when the English department developed the Iowa Writers' Workshop, a graduate program in which students earn a Master of Fine Arts in Creative Writing. Part of the program requires students to participate in a weekly fiction or poetry workshop, in which they submit a piece of creative writing, and the class discusses, or "workshops" it. These days, anyone with even fleeting aspirations of grad school writing study has had heard of—and likely envisioned themselves as members of—the Iowa workshop.

This model spread to other graduate programs, and in the late 70s a modified form made its way to high school and elementary classrooms. In a classroom workshop, a teacher often begins the workshop session with a *mini-lesson*—ten or fifteen minutes in which he or she explicitly teaches a lesson on craft, often using the work of professional writers as example. This is followed by workshop time, in which students write independently, or confer about their work with peers or with the teacher. The workshop culminates with a whole-class sharing of student work.

I used this approach in my own third grade classroom. It was a highlight of the day for me—as well as for many of my students.

Later, I encountered the workshop approach again, when I began taking writing courses at my local adult school, and through a university extension program. The workshops I attended were more relaxed than the classroom approach: basically, classes began with brief instruction from the teacher on some writing technique, and perhaps a group writing exercise. The remainder of the class, the bulk of it, consisted of considering the previously submitted work of a few students, and discussing it in depth.

In those courses I met fellow writers, and in several cases we started our own informal writing groups, meeting in each other's homes and again using the format of submitting our work to each other in advance for reading, and then meeting to discuss it.

At its most essential, the workshop approach involves gathering a group of writers to discuss one another's work. It's a fundamental part of the creative process for many adult writers, and it can be just as instructive and effective for kids.

A few benefits of a workshop:

- Workshoppers experience one of writing's essential purposes: the opportunity to convey ideas in words to an audience.
- Having an audience to write for can be highly motivating.
- A workshop audience provides feedback on one's writing. Feedback isn't always easy to come by.
- The workshop setting encourages kids to write with an audience in mind. Writing for a particular audience can help writers develop clarity in their work.
- Discussions about writing help kids learn how literature works.
- The workshop exposes kids to a variety of writing genres and styles. Very often the kids influence one another's writing.
- The workshop provides authentic deadlines for writing, which can be helpful for writers of all ages.
- A positive workshop environment can help kids recognize their personal strengths as writers.
- A workshop setting values creativity over formula, content over correctness, practice over theory—all qualities essential to developing writers.

- The workshop helps kids understand that writing is a process, that the work is malleable. Writing can always be changed and improved, if the writer chooses to.
- The workshop helps kids learn that all writers struggle, and that there are many ways to work through those difficulties.
- For homeschooled kids, the workshop provides the audience often missing in a homeschool setting. For schooled kids, the workshop allows for opportunities that may not happen in a classroom: more freedom to write creatively, and in-depth dialogue about *kid*-generated writing.
- And a benefit not to be underestimated: the workshop shows kids that writing can be fun.

My daughter enjoyed the workshop because she was with her friends and learning to write was not a painful process but was actually fun. The workshop helped her learn that what she wrote had value and people would listen to and respect whatever she wrote. —Bonnie, parent of former participant and current college student

Writer's Workshop was where my daughter "found her voice." Grammar and spelling came from her academic study, but her love of writing and her confident and oh-so-interesting style came from writing every month to share with her friends and peers in the writer's workshop. It was an invaluable ongoing experience which continues to be evidenced in her personal and academic composi-

tions. —Judith, parent of former participant and current homeschooling high school student

The Writer's Workshop format is fantastic for many reasons, and all three of my children have participated in it. The fact that my kids were free to write what interested them enabled each child to develop a "voice." I've seen how the development of my oldest son's voice as a writer made his essays in college more interesting to his professors—which has translated to As. Basically, I believe that one may teach kids to follow a format or a structure, but no one can teach them how to write with style—and that's what they learn to develop in the Writer's Workshop. —Kristin, parent of current participant and former participants currently attending high school and college

2.
WHAT TO WRITE FOR A WORKSHOP
AND HOW TO WRITE IT

In my workshops, I don't follow the traditional format used by most classroom teachers. In other words, we don't begin with a craft lesson, and we don't spend the bulk of our workshop time actually writing. Instead, we use the model I've experienced in adult writing classes: we spend most of the workshop responding to work that writers have brought from home. We do a bit of writing together at most meetings, but it isn't the focus of our gatherings.

In a school setting, it makes sense to write during the workshop, since the workshop happens on a daily, or nearly daily basis. But for a group that meets less often—weekly, bi-weekly or even monthly—it can be more practical to have participants write at home, and to devote meeting time to discussing that writing. In this way, the workshop isn't so much a stand-alone class; rather, it's an extension of, and even a celebration of, the writing kids are doing on their own. (What's that you say? Your kids don't write much on their own? Get a workshop going, and watch that begin to change!)

With this format, kids aren't restricted by what they can accomplish in a fixed meeting period. Writing at home allows kids to work in the manner they prefer: in bed late at night, or by morning in a tree house. Multiple pages while draped across a couch, or a few lines here and there in a journal left on the kitchen table. By dictating to a parent, by typing at a keyboard, or by using loopy longhand.

Bringing writing from home means that we can devote workshop time to giving one another feedback, which, as you'll see, is a rich experience.

What kids write

I like being able to write about whatever I want to write about. —Theo, 10

For me, Rule #1 in a workshop is that kids should be allowed to choose what they write about. They should feel welcome to bring writing of any genre, style and subject. This open quality helps the workshop be meaningful to kids regardless of their interests. Many kids in my workshops choose to write fiction, but I also encourage them to try nonfiction, as some discover that they prefer it. Beyond fiction, kids in my workshops have written poetry, essays, biographies, newspapers, advertisements, lists, jokes, riddles, scripts, speeches and even a song played with accompanying guitar. Occasionally they've brought papers intended for coursework elsewhere, in order to get workshop feedback on it before turning it in. (I love that they value our workshop feedback so much.)

What's especially exciting in a workshop setting is that kids inspire one another to try different types of writing. When one kid writes a parody of *If You Give a Mouse a Cookie*, subsequent meetings have other kids bringing along their own wacky versions of the story. A girl writes a story in verse and another girl moves on from her typical fiction format and tries out an edgy poem-story. Kids hear an essay about the Revolutionary War and are encouraged to try more essays, on everything from coral reefs to the film *To Kill a Mockingbird*.

You'll find more information about genres and subject matter, including difficult subject matter, in the chapters *Workshop Nitty-Gritties* and *A Crash Course in What Makes Literature Work*.

How they write it

In my workshops, we focus on the content of what kids write, not what the writing looks like. In fact, if kids are still learning the physical task of writing, I encourage parents to take dictation from their children at home, and to let the kids bring what the parent has written or typed to the workshop. This allows kids to write at a more advanced level than they might be able to on their own, and can make the writing process less tedious for a young writer.

The workshop helped my son realize that the many wonderful stories and ideas he had for writing did not have to wait until he himself was able to write them. It provided a safe and encouraging place where he could share the stories he had dictated with no embarrassment or guilt. –Jenny, parent of former participant and current college student

You can read more about taking dictation in the chapter *A Few Thoughts on Taking Dictation From Kids.*

Likewise, if kids are writing themselves for the workshop, we don't give attention to their spelling, penmanship or punctuation. In fact, we don't even see the child's writing; we only hear it read aloud. My feeling is that the workshop is not a forum for learning these mechanical skills. The workshop, rather, is a place for helping kids become excited about writing, and for helping them discover how to express themselves in words. Too much focus on mechanics tends to discourage kids from wanting to write.

My personal belief is that those writing mechanics will develop organically over time, if the child is enthused about writing. The more they write, the better they get at it—although the progress may be slower than some parents are comfortable with! I always encourage parents to allow the workshop to be a place to focus on writing content rather than appearance. This may also assure you as facilitator: if you have doubts about your own spelling, grammar and usage skills, fear not! You don't need to be a master of English to facilitate a workshop.

Often we culminate our series of workshops by making books of the kids' favorite works, or by sharing an anthology of workshop writing. See more about this in the chapter *Culminating Activities*. In this case, an audience will *see* the work, so it's appropriate to have kids work with an editor, parent or otherwise, to proofread their work and make it conventionally correct. One of the best ways for kids to learn to proofread is to print out their work and have them underline anything they suspect is incorrect. This has them taking the initial steps in the proofreading process independently; then they can work with an adult editor to fix errors.

3.
BLUEPRINT FOR A WORKSHOP

There's no single correct format for a workshop, but I'll offer the basic structure of my group's meetings, to give you a sense of what a workshop might look like. (I'll also try to anticipate questions you may have about specifics, such as meeting length and group size, in a later chapter called *Workshop Nitty-Gritties*.) Consider this a starting place, an initial blueprint. Play with the plans and create a workshop that's right for you and your particular group of kids.

What we do:

- We gather and briefly chat about how the kids' writing has fared since our last meeting.
- A child volunteers to read his or her work, or a portion of a longer work. The group responds to the work.
- We continue in this way until half of the writers have read.
- We take a short break.
- I describe a brief writing writing exploration which I've determined ahead of time. Kids work independently on the exploration.

- We reconvene and kids share what they've written for the exploration, if they choose to.
- We hear the remaining readers and offer feedback.

Let me describe each of these activities in detail.

We gather and briefly chat about how the kids' writing has fared since our last meeting.

We come together in our family room: some on furniture, some on the floor. (I always take the floor, so I don't seem too much the presider, and to show that nothing is wrong with the floor.) I ask: *So how has the writing gone? Has it been easy? Hard?* I want us to talk about the challenges: when kids couldn't come up with a topic, when they've written something that seems dull, when life has been busy and they didn't write a word until the drive over. I want to share their victories: when they've written a poem for the first time, or in the style of Terry Pratchett; when they've written something they can't wait to share, which has them bouncing on their knees, bubbling over with *please, can I go first?* My goal here is to warm up the kids and get them talking. But, perhaps more importantly, I'm hoping to establish that this is a gathering of *writers.* I want them to feel like the adults in my writing group do when we come together, commiserating and cheering because we are so grateful to be with others who understand what it means to tinker and tussle with words.

A child volunteers to read his or her work, or a portion of a longer work. The group responds to the work.

This, of course, is the heart of the workshop, and there's much to say about how you might go about it.

You may want to have a special place for the reader to sit. In classroom workshops, an "author's chair" is often placed at the front of the room. In our living room we have an oversized ottoman on which the reader sits, and the rest of us orient ourselves toward it. For younger kids, having a special spot for the reader helps them focus and listen better, I think, and sitting there to share is a point of pride. When I've worked with teens, we skip this step; kids simply read from where they happen to sit.

At the first few meetings, it can help to determine the order of readers by drawing numbers, or some other such randomizer. After that, I find that most kids are eager to share, and we simply call for volunteers. Sometimes the kids are so impatient to read that they undertake a rowdy round of Rock, Paper, Scissors to determine who *gets* to go next. (Enthusiastic readers aren't the worst raucousness you could have to endure.)

If you have a group of more than five or six, you may not have time at every meeting for each child to share. It all depends on the length of the various pieces, the depth of your group's responses, and their patience for listening. My groups tend to hover between ten and twelve participants; what works best for us is to hear half of the kids at each meeting. I send an email a few days before we meet, reminding parents—or the kids themselves, if they're old enough—whose turn it is to read on any given week. The other writers are welcome to bring work, and we often have time to hear some of those, too.

When it comes to reading aloud, writers usually read their own work. (Occasionally I've worked with fledgling readers, who choose to have a parent—or me—read their work aloud. That's fine—those writers still sit near their readers in the author's chair, and the reader moves aside when feedback is offered.) Some readers need to be reminded to read louder, or more slowly. Some need to be asked to lower their papers from their faces. I always encourage kids to practice reading their work aloud before the workshop. The quality of the reading can affect how others perceive the piece; reading aloud is a skill the workshop develops.

It may be necessary to set a time limit for readers. This becomes an issue if you have kids who write long pieces. You want to leave time for all scheduled readers; you also want to protect kids from needing to listen too long. Kids who write longer pieces can always read in installments—a bit more at each meeting. Five minutes or so is a good maximum reading time for younger kids; older kids can listen longer. I keep an eye on both the clock and the listeners' squirminess. If a reading is going on and on, I gently ask the reader to find a good place in the piece to finish up.

And then comes the time in which listeners offer feedback to the reader. Feedback is the axis on which the workshop spins, so we'll delve into it more deeply in a bit.

> *I like the workshop because it gives me a chance to write for others. The part of the workshop I like best is that I get to hear others' stories. —Cheyenne, 11*

> *The workshop gave me a place to share my writing with kids my age, which motivated me to work hard and create writing that I was proud of, and excited to share. —Lily, former workshop participant and current high school student*

We take a short break.

I've learned that kids of all ages benefit from a break midway. Younger kids listen better if they've had a chance to get up and move; older kids require socializing like oxygen, and focus better if they have some time for it. Five or ten minutes are all it takes.

I describe a brief writing exploration, which I've determined ahead of time. Kids work independently on the exploration.

My favorite part of the workshop is the writing exercise, because I love the way it challenges me. – Robin, 13

Doing a writing exploration together is optional. Many writing groups meet solely to share writing and receive feedback. However, doing a quick, impromptu writing activity gives kids a chance to try different forms than they might when composing on their own. The exploration allows them to see how a variety of writers can take the same prompt and pursue it in their own quirky styles. The exploration livens the meeting, especially for kids who might not be reading that week. Over the years, I've queried various groups on whether we might do away with the exploration to have more time for readings, and am always assaulted with a great wall of "No-o-o!" Most kids look forward to our exercises.

Explorations vary: kids might try writing lists of complaints from the perspective of an inanimate object—a bottle of ketchup, say, or a computer mouse; they might describe magical creatures in careful detail, right down to the troll's toenails; they might write a cheesy "movie trailer" for a piece they've written previously. In Part Two I'll offer a variety of suggestions for explorations, as well as resources for further inspiration.

When I first started facilitating workshops, I aimed for these exercises to be instructive, like the "mini-lessons" which classroom teachers offer during workshops. I wanted to be the quintessential English teacher (in geeky black glasses and a cardigan) teaching descriptive writing; teaching how to use active verbs; teaching how to develop nuanced characters. Over time, though, it's become more important to me that the explorations simply be fun and engaging. I've come to call them *explorations* rather than the more methodical-sounding *exercises*. Forget the vitamin-fortified, low-fat milk, I'm offering root beer! I want kids to know what it is to play with words. I want them to give-a-go new forms of writing that they might not attempt on their own. Of course, even with fun being the barometer in my exploration choice, many activities wind up being instructive as well. Probably even more so than my explicitly "educational" exercises ever were, since the kids are absorbed.

Experienced workshop kids soon begin suggesting their own ideas for explorations—sometimes variants of something we've tried, sometimes something utterly original. I try to use their suggestions if we can. Other times our feedback sessions will inspire an impromptu exercise. Recently, as we discussed use of the first and third person in response to one boy's baseball story, the conversation led what it means to write in second person. (You walk up to the plate and tap your bat on the base.) For the exploration that day, we tried writing a scene in the second person.

The exploration portion of our meeting looks like this: I encourage the kids to spread out across the downstairs rooms of our home to write, both to give them some quiet space and another chance to move. Most write independently; less fluent writers dictate to a parent-scribe. I encourage independent writers to focus on their ideas, and not to worry about spelling or penmanship, reminding them that this is always a good rule when beginning a new project. Depending on the exploration, young writers might even respond by drawing, rather than writing. With younger groups, I often fill the role of transcriber. If I'm not needed as a scribe, I'll do the exploration myself along with the kids. (Although with some groups I find myself circulating to help kids get started, or to help them stay focused.) We work silently for ten to fifteen minutes, or until most of the kids seem finished.

We reconvene and kids share what they've written for the exploration, if they choose to.

I assure kids from the first workshop that they'll never have to share their exploration work unless they choose to. Who can write creatively and off-the-cuff, knowing they'll be forced to go public with the results? Plus, the playful, experimental quality of the explorations means that not all will generate work of which the writers are proud. That's fine. Still, many kids are bursting to read their exploration work aloud. And the more trust the group accrues, the more likely kids will share their writing, even at its roughest.

We don't spend time giving intricate feedback to exploration work—we need to get back to our second group of workshop readers. Kids simply read their work aloud, and we nod in appreciation, smiling at their quirkiness, giggling when they're funny. *Uh huh,* we say. *I like that!*

We hear the remaining readers and offer feedback.

The second part of the workshop proceeds just as the first. Kids tend to get squirrely for the last few readers; I urge them to hang on until the end. Everyone winds up being last at some point, I remind, and everyone wants to share their work with enthusiastic listeners.

4.
ON OFFERING FEEDBACK

*As I received feedback from my peers, I became ac-
quainted with the importance of selling a story.
Every reaction to my work was important, but
none more so than the reinforcement of an atten-
tive group of my friends. —Henry, former
participant and current college student*

*Being with a group of people giving constructive
feedback really helped me understand more about
my own writing. Also, being the one giving feedback helped my understanding of what could be
improved in a piece of writing. —Andy, former
participant and current community college student*

Feedback can be a charged thing. It's like bacteria:
the right type is good for you, but the wrong type pro-
liferates in your gut and has you running to the toilet.
If facilitated well, feedback is what makes the kids
want to return to each workshop; it's what drives them
to pick up a pencil the night before our meeting rolls
around, if they haven't done so already. But feedback
that veers in the wrong direction can damage a group's
rapport, and can destroy a writer's confidence.

Feedback gone wrong

A friend tells a story of feedback gone wrong. During one of her first experiences facilitating a workshop, a reader asked if the other kids could give "honest" feedback on her work.

My friend tried to discourage this, but the girl was insistent. She seemed willing and eager to hear what the other kids had to say. So my friend opened up the feedback session, and she tells what happened:

"The other children began to criticize many of the things that really brought her writing to life: a lively voice, period vocabulary and little details she had created about her character's everyday life. Also, they began a string of 'you should haves.' In this case, she heard what other people would have done with the same material, but it wasn't relevant to what she was trying to do. She ended up very upset and didn't want to share her writing after that."

It's important for workshop facilitators to understand an unfortunate tenet of human nature: *Most people seem to find it easier to give negative feedback than they do positive feedback.* It's sort of a corollary to the notion that people tend to complain more often than they compliment. I've seen this play out again and again in the adult writing classes I've attended. People will start off with a few positive comments, a few niceties, a polite sniff, but then the dogs will come loose off their leashes and start attacking, pouncing on the work and shredding it. The depth of devastation depends upon the teacher's control and willingness to pull the class back. If you have a friend who has attended a grad school writing workshop, ask for such a horror story and you'll get one.

I have a trusted, beloved group of writing friends, with which I meet every few months, to discuss one another's work. As much as we women adore each other, as much as we admire each other's writing, we have to remind ourselves, aloud, meeting after meeting, to dwell a little longer in the positive. This tells me something. Considering these gentle women and their bone-deep generosity, I know that our constructive feedback isn't mean-spirited. And constructive feedback from these friends is endlessly useful to me. But why do we get pulled into the undertow of *critical* feedback so quickly? I have a theory. I think that trying to fix the work of another person is simply satisfying. It's a superficial satisfaction, of course, probably rooted in frustrations with our own writing. It's hard to write, but it's even harder to *fix* our writing. We can't quite pinpoint the flaws; we can't separate what we've attempted from what we've actually written. But it's so easy to see how we'd shape someone else's writing to our own vision! The flaws stand out, shimmering like luminescent waves, and before we realize what's happening, we're diving under, dragging down everything we think wrong with the piece. Yes, we may intend to be helpful, but ultimately it feels good to have control over someone else's writing—because we likely don't feel as if we have the same control over our own.

The good news is that a workshop doesn't have to take on this dynamic. As a facilitator, if you start your group with care, you can cultivate a positive workshop atmosphere. Kids are excellent cheerleaders. You just need to teach them the right cheers.

Dwelling on the positive

It has been great to see the kids enthusiastic about getting their writing ready for the workshop. They seemed much more interested in doing everything well because they were going to share it with the group. The positive feedback and the supportive environment was very encouraging for both of them. –Bente, parent

It was a great opportunity to take my kids to this writer's workshop year after year where they were enthusiastic and I knew they were learning skills that would help them the rest of their lives. It was such a positive setting. –Deborah, parent of former participants

I encourage you to allow only positive feedback in your workshops for a while. Perhaps that sounds overly touchy-feely; perhaps you worry that strictly positive feedback can't help writers develop.

You might be surprised. Positive feedback is probably more powerful than you imagine.

First, if we want to enthuse kids about writing, we should make writing as easy, stress-free and pleasurable as possible. Writing is difficult enough; we don't want to confound the process. In his book *Holding on to Good Ideas in a Time of Bad Ones: Six Literacy Principles*

Worth Fighting For, Thomas Newkirk writes, "The act of writing is so full of stopping points that it is easy for negative voices to infiltrate the process—insinuating that we are saying nothing new, that the writing is awkward, simplistic, just plain bad…In some cases, these critical voices are versions of parental ones, or teacherly ones, or they may just be parts of temperaments prone to self-criticism…Whatever the reason, the voices in our heads are often ones that do not help us much." Let's hope that the kids in your group haven't already been beaten down by discouragers and margin-writing teachers with red pens. You certainly don't want negative feedback received at your workshop to provide those taunting voices.

Peter Elbow, in *Writing With Power*, shares similar insight. Consider that he offers the following advice to adult writers: "Until you are secure in your writing—until, that is, you know you can produce lots of writing whenever you need it and that some of it will be good or can be made good—stick with plain sharing and noncritical feedback." If novice adult writers need to be coddled from critical feedback as Elbow suggests, surely nascent-writer kids do!

Don't think of positive feedback simply as a benign substitute for critical feedback, however. Positive feedback can be highly instructive in its own right. A workshop can cultivate the positive voices in the head that a writer needs. If writers are reminded, workshop after workshop, of their true strengths, they will begin to internalize those strengths. They'll begin to believe that, yes, they are masters of compelling dialogue, or that they have a way with the humorous random detail, or that they're skilled memoirists who manage to make tales of trips to the recycling center entertaining. When the writing gets difficult, a young writer might think: the kids in my workshop say my stuff is funny, so I know I can write something funny. How did I do it the last time?

Years ago, I took a writing class at my local adult school, taught by a woman named Charlotte Cook. I think I paid sixty dollars for a ten-week course, and it may have been the best sixty dollars I've ever spent, because Charlotte was one of the finest writing teachers I've ever watched in action. Over the years I've taken a collection of much more expensive writing courses through university extension programs and the like, but no instructor ever pulled off the magic that Charlotte did in a high school Civics classroom each Wednesday night. She had a gift for pinpointing the strengths in any writer's work, no matter how unpracticed those writers were. The nutty psychotherapist whose mysteries strayed aimlessly learned that she had an ear for dialogue; the quiet young mother who timidly shared her personal essays discovered that her lines had the lilt of poetry. Charlotte helped me understand for the first time that I had a knack for choosing details, which has kept me searching for the right ones ever since. Sometimes I'd listen to a classmate's contribution for the week and think *what will Charlotte possibly find good in that?* And then Charlotte would find something. She didn't dwell on what our work lacked, the way teachers in my other courses seemed to do; instead, she kept digging into the garage sale heaps of our drafts and drawing out treasures, with a big grin on her face. Sometimes the treasures were small, no bigger than napkin rings, but they were enough to keep us writing, and polishing, until we slowly began to recognize, on our own, where our words had worth.

As a facilitator of workshops, I've always tried to emulate Charlotte's treasure digging.

Positive feedback gives a writer more than just confidence; it gives us a sense of how to proceed. If we know what we're doing well, we're likely to keep doing it. Our strengths as writers are not always obvious from where we sit behind the pen or the keyboard, but having them proclaimed and explained in a workshop setting begins to establish and solidify them. They become like handholds on a climbing wall: once we have a solid footing in one area, we can creep to that next spot, just a little farther up, and take a new risk in our writing. Positive feedback offers a map of where to begin, and suggestions for where to go. Too much critical feedback, on the other hand, simply gives a map of spots to avoid, labeled with skulls and crossbones. It's hard to get anywhere when you're just trying to keep out of trouble.

Many of us make it to adulthood with no sense of our own strengths as writers—we may not recognize that we write with clarity, or sensitivity, or that we've inherited our crazy cowboy grandfather's knack for spinning a gripping tale. Yet in a workshop environment, kids gain a sense of their strengths from the start.

How to give positive feedback

Imagine that you're nine years old. You're reading your first piece of writing to your new workshop group—a story about a group of zombies out to eat the brains of the reader of said story. You've just read your final line: *Guess it's time to eat your brains now.* You look up from the page and wait for feedback.

But the kids don't say anything. They don't know what to say. They're worrying about what to comment on, weighing out different parts of the story and trying to choose a favorite. They fiddle with the Velcro on their shoes, the barrettes in their hair, thinking, while you dissolve in the silence, wishing you'd stayed at home, watching old episodes of Scooby Doo on YouTube.

This is where the magic words *I remember* come in.

I always ask the listening kids to start a feedback session simply remembering details from the piece. Actually, after the reader finishes, we clap for the piece—which kills off the pesky silence with a boom. Then everyone with feedback raises his or her hand, and the reader calls on us, one at a time. (I like to give this role to the reader, rather than myself as facilitator, to give the child ownership of the feedback session.) We listeners simply remember what we just heard. Classroom teachers often call this *receiving* the piece— the goal is simply for the group to acknowledge that they've been listening. It gets the feedback session started right away: there's no awkward lag as listeners formulate their thoughts, and weigh their likings. They simply need to recall a detail.

The truth is that there is often something to be learned from those recalled details. Kids remember that the zombie boss was named Zomboss, or how the girl cartwheeled out of bed in another story, or the line about coffee grounds that splayed from a mass into bits in another because those details are memorable. Often, more than one child will remember the same detail— and I always tell the kids that's it's helpful to mention when they've noticed the same detail as someone else. This tells the writer that the detail was particularly resonant.

Recalling those details will warm up the responders, and will almost always lead, organically, to mentions of what they liked in the piece.

As useful as *I remember* feedback is as an icebreaker, it doesn't offer much substance to the writer. You'll also want to encourage the more specific feedback that I'll describe in the next section. In time, if you find that your group isn't moving beyond *I remember* feedback— some kids fall back on it because it's easy—you may want to wean them from the practice.

You like me!

There's that *like* word. In theory, when giving feedback, it's a good idea to stay away from phrases such as *I liked*, which is a judgment, and try to give more objective responses such as *I noticed that you started your essay with a story.* Writing to please others shouldn't be the ultimate goal of the workshop, yet if everyone prefaces their feedback with *I liked*, kids might get that impression. That's the theory, anyway. In reality, when kids are enthusiastic about another kid's writing, it's pretty much impossible for them not to preface their comments with *I liked*. Being a kid is all about being eager and animated and liking what you like! Asking kids not to use the word is akin to asking them not to sneeze. They can't help themselves. In fact, you yourself may have a hard time not using the word *like*—but try. Experiment with modeling alternatives such as *I noticed* or *I remembered*. Also, attempt to use the word *effective* rather than *good* (another judging word.) Then again, if striking *I liked* from your group's feedback vocabulary is simply too awkward and difficult, let it slide. *Like* all you like. After all, what works and doesn't work in a piece of writing is largely a matter of reader taste—his or her likes and dislikes. (On the other hand, quash the phrase *I didn't like* immediately, as if it were a cockroach that scuttled into your workshop. More on the hows and whys of that later.)

But *liking* something in a workshop shouldn't be as easy as clicking on an upturned Facebook thumb. Nope, when kids say they like something, I prompt them to tell why—because this is what the writer needs to hear, and because it helps the speaker learn to give more nuanced feedback. When a boy says he likes the main character in one girl's story about a school for thieves, I nudge him to tell more—until he comes up with, "She's funny. And she's lazy. And she likes to eat pineapple with tuna fish." Sometimes it takes kids a moment or two to pinpoint the reasons for their likes, but helping them put those appreciations into words is worth the wait—for both the reader and the speaker.

The golden line

Often, when a kid reads at the workshop, you'll hear a sentence that snags your attention, that compels you to copy it down. Some writing educators call such sentences *golden lines*. I'm not sure where the phrase originated, but I first encountered it in Ralph Fletcher's writing guide for kids, *Live Writing: Breathe Life Into Your Words*. After sharing a golden line from a favorite picture book, Fletcher writes, "A sweet sentence like that makes you sit up straight, go back, and read it all over again."

A golden line is a sentence—or a part of a sentence—that has something special. It might surprise the reader with unexpected words, or a particularly apt analogy. It might contain a verb used in uncharacteristic way. A golden line is fresh and original. A thirteen-year-old in one of my workshops wrote, "All the years I had spent in the back of the shop, hidden away from the world, had perfected my piping skills until creating the intricate flowers and vines had become easier than even writing my own name." Comparing cake-piping to writing her name has special resonance in this particular story, because the character's central conflict is that she doesn't know her true identity. It's a golden line.

Help the kids in your workshop begin to recognize golden lines in the work of others. You could introduce the idea by reading a few golden lines selected from literature, but I prefer to let the notion evolve from the kids' work. I simply describe a golden line as a special sentence that makes you stop and want to hear it again. I point out a golden line or two during a feedback session. Immediately the kids follow suit. Some may surprise you with their skill at recognizing extraordinary writing.

Often, many kids will agree that a particular line is golden, which is evidence to the writer that he or she has written an effective sentence. Other times kids debate which of several lines is most golden. These are good conversations to have! In order to make a case for a particular line, kids must dig into the specifics of what makes that line work so well. In doing so, they develop their intuition and knowledge of what makes good writing.

Not every work contains a golden line. That's okay. The more kids begin to recognize beautiful writing, and to hear it being recognized, the harder they may try to create remarkable lines of their own.

It can be fun to introduce a special pen along with the idea of a golden line—a yellow highlighter, perhaps, or even a metallic golden pen. When a writer or listeners have deemed a line golden, the writer may choose to highlight or underline the line with the special pen. This offers a tangible reminder of what good writing looks like.

You can also ask kids to hunt for golden lines in their own work before their workshop readings. This may help them consider how an audience will interpret their work—and it might encourage them to tinker a bit longer, to try crafting special sentences.

As I've said previously in this guide, it's a great gift for a writer to understand what he or she is doing well. In his book *Several Short Sentences About Writing*, Verlyn Klinkenborg writes about the feeling writers get when they when they recognize that a line they've written is special:

> Even beginning writers notice this.
> Learning that feeling is important.
> It's a guide and an incentive to making more
> good sentences.

If your workshop does nothing more than encourage kids to make more good sentences, you will not have wasted your time.

Useful feedback prompts for listeners:

- "I remember _____."
- "I was intrigued by _____ because _____."
- "I noticed when you used the word _____ because _____."
- "Your piece reminded me of _____ because _____."

You might consider posting these where kids can see them during a feedback session.

You can also model using these prompts yourself. Yes, the facilitator can and should give feedback. But try not to elevate your feedback as if it's more important than the kids'. To ensure this, make sure that several kids respond before you do—but don't save your feedback until last, either. When you have something to say, raise your hand, just as the kids do, and wait for the reader to call on you. Naturally, I often go into more depth with my feedback, but I still try to take on the role of one commenter among many. I want the kids to learn to value the insight of other kids, and not to direct all their attention to me.

Many kids, especially younger ones, seem quite satisfied with basic, positive feedback. They seem content to simply share their work and have it appreciated. Not having plans to revise, they don't care to know how their work might be improved. (We'll reflect more on revision and the effects of age later.) Still, it can't hurt to help writers consider the possibilities their work might hold. That's where constructive feedback comes in.

Overheard at the workshop—a sampling of actual feedback from kids:

"I thought you did a good job explaining what was going on for someone who doesn't play Magic."

"I liked how you phrased things. When the cowboy was talking, it really sounded like how someone from Texas would talk."

"You don't expect gory messes in a If You Give a Mouse a Cookie *story. I thought that was funny and surprising."*

"The words you used in their dialogue was funny, and it made them seem particularly dumb, which was great: lame, nifty, waz up, omg."

"I didn't think it was going to end that way. It was…satisfying."

Feedback that builds

construct: *v.* 1. to build

constructive: *adj.* 2. having the quality of contributing helpfully

So when did *constructive feedback* become a synonym for *criticism.* It has. Have you noticed?

I suppose it makes sense. If you have two types of feedback, and one is positive, than the other type would presumably be its opposite: negative. But negative feedback is not what we're going for in a workshop setting, and it isn't a phrase you'd want to use with your workshop kids.

Instead, let's go back to the definitions of *construct* and *constructive.* At the roots of these words are notions of building and helping. Constructive feedback should be input that helps a writer expand the work at hand. That helps the writer approach the work like a contractor: renovating what could use improving, and adding on where some extra space would be useful. I like to refer to this sort of input as *building feedback*—it helps the writer build on to what he or she has so far. (And it steers clear of the negative connotations that the phrase *constructive feedback* has picked up on the side of the road over the years.)

Basically, we simply use the term *feedback* to describe encouragement for the writing as it is, while *building feedback* provides options for expanding the writing.

After kids have had a few sessions with purely basic feedback, try moving them into building feedback. I wouldn't make a big deal of this shift. I wouldn't start a workshop announcing, *This week we're going to try a different type of feedback!* Kids are smart: they'll suspect that something's up and that the new babysitter who showed up with lollipops is about to introduce a chore chart. Avoid that. Instead, simply try posing a new question or two during feedback time.

Try, for example, asking if there were any parts in the piece that listeners would like to know more about. Or, ask if there were parts that confused them. You could add these to your list of prompts.

Useful building feedback prompts for listeners:

- "I'd like to know more about _____."
- "I'm confused about _____."

These prompts work because they're fairly non-threatening to the writer. They open the door to revision without seeming critical. Hearing what kids would like to know more about can come across as a compliment—*more of this, please!* —while at the same time it gives the writer ideas for expansion. Likewise, discussion of confusing parts helps the writer begin to see a piece through the eyes of a reader, but the feedback is specific and concrete enough that it doesn't feel like an attack.

I find that these two prompts are enough to get a good *building* discussion going. As a facilitator, you'll want to stay on top of these discussions, and be ready to tug back on the leash if the talk turns. If anyone utters something along the lines of *I didn't like*, stop that speaker immediately. Gently remind that such feedback can be unhelpful to the reader, and try to help the speaker rephrase the comment more objectively.

Overheard at the workshop—a sampling of building feedback from kids:

"I wondered why he was so interested in the baby tortoise when there was that giant dragon there."

" I was really curious about why she ignores everybody. I wondered if she couldn't hear, or if something is wrong with her."

"I found it interesting that the snatchers couldn't get the kids. I wanted to know more about that."

"I liked the dialogue, but it was hard to tell who was talking because the different characters' words went all together."

"I liked the parts where you explained why you thought that about video games. It would be interesting if you did that for all your ideas."

Put the writer in control

Younger kids and more novice writers often don't seem terribly interested in building feedback. Still, it's worth spending a little time with the prompts above, so kids gradually get a sense that writing is malleable, and can be changed and improved. On the other hand, older kids, and younger ones who are particularly avid writers, are more eager for this sort of feedback. As soon as they get to a point in which they want to revise their writing, building feedback becomes essential.

The two previous prompts will continue to be helpful for these kids, but you can go deeper into building feedback by asking the writer a single, simple question:

"Do you have any questions for us?"

I always end a feedback session with this question. Younger, less established writers often defer, or ask a simple question such as, "Do you think I should continue this story?" More advanced writers, however, often take the cue and run with it. They become quite adept at getting the feedback they need, coming up with questions such as, "Do you think this was a likable character?" "Did the ending seem realistic to you?" "Should I start the essay like I did, or do you have a better idea for a beginning?"

I often suggest that kids think through and scribble down their questions at home. The longer kids participate in the workshop, the better they get at asking these questions, which helps shape the workshop to their specific needs. This keeps feedback sessions from becoming too listener-directed, and devolving into critical, let-us-rewrite-your-work-for-you sessions.

Consider the cone of silence

Another option for shaping feedback, especially for older kids, is to institute what one of my extension course instructors called "The Cone of Silence." Immediately after the writer has read his or her work, and the group has clapped, an invisible cone drops and mutes the reader until the end of the feedback session. This approach can be effective for several reasons. First, if listeners are confused about any part of the story, the writer's silence forces them to work together to tease out what confused them. These discussions can be highly instructive. The writer will hear how different readers interpreted the piece, which can highlight any problems. On the other hand, if the writer is allowed to jump in early and explain, the conversation is cut off, and the writer doesn't get a full picture of how the work is affecting readers.

Additionally, if a writer is able to speak during a feedback session, the session often lingers on and gets bogged down, as the writer continually explains and defends what he or she tried to do in the piece. Instead, ask the writer to save those comments until the end of the feedback session, when the cone comes off. At that point the writer can also ask those essential, previously-mentioned questions of listeners.

You can also try this with younger kids, but I find that they tend to get hung up and distracted by keeping the writer quiet, rather than the conversation at hand. Lots of pointed fingers and admonishments: "Don't talk! You can't talk!" With younger groups, it can be easier to simply ask the writer to withhold commentary as needed, if listeners seem to be working together to tease apart something in the piece at hand.

A round of applause—or two

I lead my groups to applaud twice for the reader. Once, as I mentioned, after he or she has read the piece, which bridges the awkward silence before kids raise their hands with feedback. And again, when the feedback session is finished, and the writer leaves the author's chair—almost always grinning, sometimes sheepishly. You can never have too much applause. And you can never be over-appreciated when you're a writer.

5.

TIPS FOR THE FACILITATOR

Or, how to dig for treasure like Charlotte Cook.

But first I must offer a disclaimer. Perhaps you do not want to dig for treasure like Charlotte. Perhaps the thought of *facilitating* or *teaching* in any way makes you nervous. Fear not. If all you do is host a workshop, gathering kids and making sure they are kind to each other, you will accomplish wonders. That's all it really takes. Just giving kids a place to share their writing and chat about it will likely excite and motivate them unlike anything else you may have tried.

If, however, you'd like to gently guide the discussions a little deeper, I have some tips.

Take notes as kids read.

Jot down words and phrases that capture your attention. It's much easier to recall specific details—a lively verb, a quirky character name—if you record them. Maybe there's a section that you'd like the writer to re-read during feedback time, so the group can discuss it; scrawl down something to remind you where to return. I also encourage older, fluent writers to try taking notes as well. Doesn't work for all of them, but it does for some.

Remember that your feedback doesn't have to be teacher-ish.

Sometimes it can get a tad nerve-wracking when you're facilitating, and you feel pressured to say something. Worse when you feel that your feedback should be particularly insightful. It doesn't have to be. Remember my advice that you don't necessarily want to draw attention to your feedback, and elevate it above the kids' feedback? It's perfectly okay to simply raise your hand and offer an *I remember* if that's all you can come up with.

Simply notice what captures your attention as a child reads, and try to pinpoint why it captivated you.

There's usually something that stands out, though it may be a small something. A word. A phrase. A line of dialogue. Write it down, and try to figure out why it compels. It's best not to let your mind wander as a child reads, but there's time for some flash analysis when the group claps for the reader, and as the first few listeners raise their hands. You may surprise yourself with how insightful you become with practice.

Learn a little something about how literature works.

I'm simply talking about paying attention to the items in a writer's toolbox. The tricks that make a piece of writing move a reader. A teacher might call these tools and tricks *literary elements*. Don't be cowed by such a phrase. Truth is, anybody who has spent a respectable amount of time reading and being read to has likely intuited many of these elements—and this goes for the kids as well as you. Start discussing a ten-year-old's story about a dragon and kids may mention that they liked the "talking parts" (because the writer has a knack for *dialogue*) or that the part about the baby dragon was interesting (because the *description* was so effective.) You may be rusty on the terminology, but you know what makes writing enthralling. In an upcoming chapter, I'll give a crash course in what makes literature work so you have the language to back up your intuitions, which will be useful in your discussions with the kids.

If, however, the notion of studying elements of literature overwhelms you and makes you feel that this workshop thing is more than you had in mind, that it might be easier to facilitate a course in Rune Carving, in Finnish, then shelve that section for a few months and revisit it later. Your workshop will be just fine.

6.
WORKSHOP NITTY-GRITTIES

How many kids should I invite?

This depends on how many interested kids you know, and the size of group you're comfortable with. A group as small as three can be effective, if the kids are enthusiastic and cooperative with each other. I've worked with groups as large as twelve, but it takes effort to manage the energy of such a big group, especially if the kids are younger than teenagers. If it's your first time facilitating, you might aim for somewhere between five and eight participants—enough kids for variety in writing and feedback, but not so many that there will be too much listening required, and too much energy to manage.

You can always start small and invite more kids as you go.

How old should the kids be? And how much can they range in age?

Kids of almost any age can participate in a workshop. The first time I hosted one, I invited several kids from seven to ten years old. Many of them had younger, four or five-year old siblings. Another mom did separate activities for these kids in another room, but after a few weeks, the younger kids became intrigued with what their older siblings were doing, and sat in on a workshop session. They loved it and wanted to participate too! They began to bring work that they'd dictated to parents at home. Many couldn't yet read themselves; their parents sat beside them at the author's chair and read the writing aloud. Then the child would receive feedback. These younger kids became some of our most eager participants, and I continued to work with many of them into their teens.

Bottom line: even very young kids can enjoy a workshop. As do kids of every other age group, up through adults! Teens in particular gain much from a workshop setting; at their age they really begin to value feedback and eagerly incorporate it into their work.

Regarding ranges in age: again, this depends on you and the particular kids. One year I facilitated a poetry workshop of five girls who were all the same age, and it was lovely. Other times, as in that first workshop, I've worked kids who were up to five years apart. A smaller age range is easier, because there will be fewer developmental differences in the kids, but groups with bigger ranges have their benefits too. With that first workshop, the older kids modeled sophisticated writing for the younger ones, and also offered nuanced feedback. The younger kids contributed energy and enthusiasm to the group. They were almost always the first to offer feedback, especially when the older kids went through their *I'm-too-cool* phase as preteens. With this group, many parents attended along with the kids; they were able to help the younger ones with the exploration portion of the meeting, and they helped keep the kids focused.

Give thought to the particular kids you're considering for your group. If their ages are widely ranged, you may do best with older kids who are fairly patient, and younger ones who are somewhat mature for their age.

Where do you gather?

We meet in the family room of our home. I shift a few chairs and a table so there's room for everyone to gather. We don't have enough furniture for all the kids to have a spot on sofa or chair, so some of us have to take to the floor. (As I mentioned, I always take the floor, to minimize my role as facilitator, and to show the kids that the floor isn't bad.) We have an ottoman that serves as our Author's Chair, and we all orient ourselves toward it when someone reads. You could, I suppose, gather around a table for meetings, especially with older kids and teens. But I find that a more freeform gathering space works well: kids often shift their spots during our meetings, slipping from the sofa to the floor, or stretching out across the carpet. Being able to move a bit, while still listening, helps them stay focused, I think. More on that in a bit.

I know others who have used a gathering space in a library or church. That can work well too. One consideration in such a setting is the noise level. Can kids clap and respond with enthusiasm, or is there an expectation of quiet? Is there somewhere to run and release energy during a break? If not, shorter meetings might be a good idea in such a space.

What should kids bring along?

I ask kids to bring a pen or pencil, and either a notebook or a folder with blank paper inside. And a copy of their writing, of course. I always have pencils and paper available, but scrounging enough decent (read: sharpened, un-chewed and eraser-tipped) pencils for everyone makes me a little nuts, so I appreciate when kids bring their own.

Some years the kids and I have created writer's notebooks together, taking composition books and dividing them, as each kid desires, into sections with titles such as "Interesting Words", "Quotes", "Writing Ideas," and "Play", which is a section for recording our explorations and other experimental writing. Those plastic, sticky page tabs that you can buy at stationary stores work wonderfully for divvying up and labeling composition books. I encourage kids to add to their notebooks at home, and to bring them to our meetings. Sometimes we share bits from our notebooks, and discuss ways to make the notebooks more useful. If creating notebooks with your workshop kids is an intriguing idea, I recommend Ralph Fletcher's *The Writer's Notebook* for further inspiration.

How often should we meet?

As often as you can! Weekly would be ideal, but busy schedules don't always allow for that. My groups generally meet every two weeks, which keeps the momentum going, but doesn't feel like too much of a burden to me as host and facilitator. When I've worked with teens, we've met monthly due to their busy schedules, but we spent time reading their work and responding in writing between meetings. (More on that later.)

How long should a meeting run?

Depends on the number of kids, their ages, and their ability to listen. Younger kids in a smaller group of, say, three or four, might accomplish plenty in an hour; a larger group requires more time for more readers. With my current group of twelve 9-13 year-olds, we began with hour-and-a-half meetings and quickly increased to two hours to allow for enough readings, a break and a writing exploration. By the end of the two hours, listening becomes quite challenging for many of them, and they bust out of my house like so many loosed champagne corks! With teens, I've started with two-hour meetings and increased to two-and-a-half, at the kids' request. If in doubt, begin with a shorter time period than you think you'll need, explaining to parents that meeting times might lengthen if the kids want it.

Should parents stay and participate in the workshop?

First off, I can't really express what a screaming privilege it felt like to sit and listen to the kids' writing. They were so open and it was like getting a peek inside their heads, which can be rare even for a homeschooling mom. So that was a big part for me—I sort of felt like I was at writing church. —Stefani, parent

This is up to you. I've always invited parents of younger kids to stay, but haven't required it. It can be helpful to have parents experience the workshop, so they can help bring home what kids learn, and extend it to at-home writing and reading discussions. If parents stay, I ask them to listen as the kids do, and participate in offering feedback. It can be very useful to have the insightful feedback of other adults, so long as parents don't monopolize feedback sessions. The kids' feedback should remain the focus of the workshop. In my group, some parents attend every week, some attend occasionally, and some never stay. Consider your role as facilitator: would it be helpful to have other parents stay and help out, or would it make you feel more self-conscious in your facilitating role? You could always ask parents to stay for an initial meeting, and then make your decision from there.

With my teen groups, I've never had parents stay—except for our end-of-the-year reading celebrations. Teens, as you might expect, seem to appreciate writing without adults reading over their shoulders.

I've always felt honored by the teens' willingness to share with me, as facilitator.

What should we do at the first meeting?

I ask kids to bring writing to the first meeting *only if they want to*. (More on requiring kids to bring writing coming up.) Usually, you'll find a few kids who are eager to bring something to that first meeting, who will get the group going; others may need to experience the workshop before they're ready to share. I encourage parents to tell kids they can bring something short and simple. Writing a list, for example, can be an approachable form for many kids; they might bring lists of how to bother a sibling, or how to win at Monopoly–or why they dislike writing!

You might consider starting your first meeting by reading a brief, engaging picture book, chosen according to the group at hand, and responding to it together, as if it were writing brought by a workshop participant. Have feedback prompts posted for kids to refer to. This gives kids the opportunity to test out the feedback format, without putting a child on the spot.

Do you require kids to bring writing to the workshop?

I do. At least after they've attended one meeting. I think it's important that if kids are attending and offering feedback on the work of others, that they are contributing themselves. When I first started facilitating workshops, I allowed kids to attend without sharing their own work, thinking that it would be beneficial not to pressure them. A few kids, however, never found the confidence to bring anything. And the longer they went without contributing, the higher the pressure built for them to bring something "worth" sharing; they eventually dropped out of the workshop altogether. So I've learned to require kids to bring *something* in order to participate, and have stressed the notion that they don't need to bring writing that is lengthy or polished.

As mentioned earlier, with a large group you may not have time for kids to share something at every meeting. For my groups, kids are scheduled to bring something to every other meeting. They're always welcome to bring work to the meetings in between, and we often find time to hear these extra pieces. Sometimes kids don't bring work on the weeks in which they're scheduled, which means that they've missed their turn. This is generally disappointing enough to encourage them to have something for the next time they're scheduled. Families are busy, though, and sometimes kids just don't have work to share. I wouldn't worry about that, but if kids repeatedly show up empty-handed, you may want to talk to the parent, and reconsider the child's participation in the group. There's nothing more disappointing than gathering kids for a workshop, and not having enough work to discuss.

Should there be writing topics that are off-limits?

I don't set limits on what kids can write. Rather, I've always assumed that I would deal with any subject matter that made me, or other participants, feel uncomfortable on a case-by-case basis. In more than twelve years of workshops, I don't recall having to talk to a child about having written something that seemed inappropriate for our group.

Often in classrooms, students are not allowed to write work that is violent, or based on popular culture, such as television programs, movies or videogames. I urge you to consider refraining from making such rules in your workshop—particularly because writing related to violence, adventure, fantasy, action heroes, videogames and the like tends to be attractive to many boys. In his book *Boy Writers,* Ralph Fletcher lists results from a teacher survey asking which topics boys preferred to write about when given choice. It's a long list that runs from aliens to wars to accidents to action figures to robots and video games-- subjects "heavy on action and conflict." After twelve years of workshops, I would echo that many of the boys I've known are also drawn to such topics. Not exclusively, but consistently. Just this past year, my own ten-year-old son wrote a story of a boy trapped in a videogame, another about two boys who hunt monsters, a fantasy battle scene populated with orcs and trolls, a list of reasons kids should be allowed to play video games, and the tale of a Colossus who showed up at a Whole Foods Market—

to name just a few. Clearly there's a magnetism to this sort of action and adventure for some boys! In *Boy Writers*, Fletcher writes, "…I would argue that if you outlaw all 'boy topics' you end up with a very watered-down menu, at least from a boy's point of view…which creates a more serious problem—a room full of turned-off boys."

I agree. If you want the kids in your workshop to be enthusiastic about their writing, see if you can allow them to write about whatever excites them, so long as it doesn't upset anyone. If something comes up that you or others are uncomfortable with, you can always talk to the child and/or his or her parents privately.

How do you deal with kid energy?

It can be tough for kids to sit still, listening, for long chunks of time! A mid-workshop break can be essential. I always encourage younger kids to head out to our backyard to run during breaks. (And quietly wish we had a trampoline for them to jump on.) Also, as I mentioned, I encourage them to move to different downstairs rooms in our home when completing the session's writing exploration. This gets them up and moving, and gives them more space to spread out. Kids often elect to work on the exploration while sprawled over carpets or couches. That's fine by me! Naturally, they get more silly and unfocused towards the end of the workshop; we make sure to shift up the order of readers so the same kids don't get those less desirable, end-of-the-meeting reading slots. Then again, if a majority of kids seem to lose it towards the end of every meeting, consider shortening your meetings by half-an-hour, or even fifteen minutes.

Know too, that just because kids are wiggly, it doesn't mean they aren't listening. In my current workshop, one of the most active kids, the one who likes to grip the back of our leather chair and dangle his full weight from his fingertips during readings, is the same kid who can repeat, verbatim, long lines from other kids' work.

Generally, I'd say, the kids are eager to listen to one another's writing. They don't wiggle because they're bored; they wiggle because they're kids. As facilitator, you'll want to learn to work with that.

What if a particular child is repeatedly disruptive during the workshop?

As facilitator, I prefer to work with kids who *want* to be at the workshop. I understand that some parents might want their child to attend because the workshop seems like a good idea, just as eating kale seems like a good idea. But if the kid doesn't want to be there, you're headed for trouble. I always invite unsure kids to try the workshop out for a few sessions, assuring them that they can discontinue attending if it isn't for them, and my feelings won't be hurt.

If a kid *wants* to be at the workshop, but is still disruptive, you have more leverage. In that case, I'd speak with the child, and possibly the parent, and discuss how the behavior is affecting others. A child may be willing to work harder to listen if the workshop matters to him or her. Having the parent attend the workshop might help. Then again, some kids are simply not developmentally ready or personally suited to the workshop setting. If a particular child is undermining the workshop, you shouldn't feel obligated to have him or her continue. You could always ask that child to take a break from the workshop and possibly try again after a time.

Know, too, that your own child is likely to be the most disruptive in the crowd. At least that's what I've found after twelve years of workshops. It makes sense: your kids are at home, they feel comfortable with you and the setting and sometimes like to assert their dominion over *their* kingdom! Luckily, my three kids have all loved the workshop, and have responded, for the most part, to my private requests for more reined-in workshop behavior. I've also simply gritted my teeth and tried to cut my kids some slack: they're sharing their parent and their home with a bunch of other kids, and that isn't always easy.

What if some kids don't offer feedback to others?

Some kids in your workshop will love giving feedback while others only will do it begrudgingly. Some will offer thoughtful, sophisticated insights; some will offer only cursory responses. Often, feedback sessions are fueled by the enthusiasm of the same handful of kids. To a degree, you need to accept that kids have different strengths and challenges. Still, I believe that if kids are taking part in a workshop, they have a duty to offer feedback to others. I ask kids to try to give at least one piece of feedback to each reader. The kids who don't enjoy giving feedback are likely fall back on simple *I remember* feedback, but at least they're participating.

If it seems that some kids are routinely refraining from participating in our feedback sessions, it can be helpful to talk about it to the group, without using names. Discuss why feedback is useful. Ask what it might feel like to read one's work to the group and have no one respond to it. The kids who don't offer feedback generally expect to receive it; a discussion may help those kids understand that this is unfair. Sometimes kids just need a little reminder that they need to participate.

If a group discussion doesn't help, you may want to talk to an individual child privately. Explain that you notice that the child hasn't been giving feedback, and ask why. I've had some kids tell me that they don't know how to respond to some pieces, especially if they don't like them. In which case I challenge them to listen for one small thing that each writer is doing well, maybe one little detail, and to share that. Other kids feel awkward about giving feedback, and need a little help in learning how to do it. Then again, you may have a child in your workshop who simply refuses to give feedback. In that case you may want to talk to the child's parent. A workshop may not be the best forum for that child.

What about kids who just don't like the workshop?

The workshop isn't for everyone. Honestly, in the years I've facilitated, I've been surprised and delighted at the high ratio of kids who've come to love and be inspired by the workshop setting. (Which has me lapsing into hyperbole and tossing around words like *magical*.) Still, over the years I've come across a handful of kids for whom the format didn't work. Some didn't like the pressure of having to write, some didn't enjoy sharing their work with others, some didn't like listening to the work of others, some simply couldn't endure such a structured activity. Who knows why the workshop works for some kids and not for others? I always start a new workshop with a trial period, assuring kids and parents that individuals can gracefully withdraw if the workshop turns out to be not for them.

As facilitator, try not to take it personally if a child chooses not to continue. The workshop setting doesn't inspire everyone.

Why don't kids revise their work after getting feedback in the workshop?

This is a question that nettled me for years. I'd hear kids receive insightful feedback from other kids; I'd even see them get excited about that feedback. But would they go back and make revisions to their work? Nope. At least not very often. They'd just forge ahead with the next installment of their writing, or with a different piece altogether. This drove me a little crazy, especially with my own kids. Wasn't the point of the workshop to get feedback, and to let that feedback inform their writing?

I came to understand that revision is somewhat developmental. Younger kids write, are happy with their writing, and they're *finished*. Most don't want to linger with something they've already written. Over time, though, I began to see that even if kids didn't revise the work at hand, they often applied workshop feedback to later writing. When workshop kids request more dialogue in a story, for example, a young writer might not go back and add dialogue to that particular story, but her next story might have more dialogue. In *But How Do You Teach Writing?* Barry Lane summarizes this notion well: "It is important for young writers to see the possibility of revision in their work, even if they revise their story by writing a new one."

I've also had the lucky experience of working with several kids over the course of many years, from their childhoods into their teens. Guess what happened when they became teenagers? They began to use workshop feedback to revise their work! They even began bringing their revisions to share at the workshop! By choice! It was as if they'd reached a new developmental stage where lingering with their work and shaping it became fulfilling. (Talk about *fulfilling*: as their long-time workshop facilitator, I was elated.)

Barry Lane also offers this wisdom: "I believe students truly learn to revise when they do it on their own.

When a student says a piece of writing is done, it is. Our job as teachers is to help them to see on their own that it isn't." If the kids in your workshop don't seem to be revising their work, take heart. They're likely revising their ideas about writing—and one day they may even revise their written words.

> *That was the part of the writing workshop that I looked forward to the most: the safe, constructive atmosphere to grow our writing, or even to get a few new ideas for next steps. —Ingrid, former participant and current college student*

I'm nervous about committing to a workshop. What if it doesn't go well?

First, you may want to find another parent or two, and facilitate the workshop cooperatively. That's one way to take the pressure off of a single facilitator.

You could also start with a short workshop series. Schedule a run of three or four workshops to see how it goes. A single workshop won't allow enough time for kids to relax and settle into a routine, but three or four meetings will be a good start. Know that it takes many more meetings for kids to really gel into a group, but after a handful of meetings you'll be able to tell if a longer series is worth committing to. My groups usually run from fall through spring, meeting twice a month, and breaking for the summer.

7.
CULMINATING ACTIVITIES

After having a series of workshops, it can be fun to celebrate. Since my groups usually take a summer break, we always have a party for our last meeting. Some possibilities:

A book-making party

This can be especially fun for younger kids. Each child chooses a favorite piece he or she has shared during the workshop, or a collection of pieces, and makes a book of it. In my workshops we've made fairly elaborate books with stitched-in pages and hard covers. Before our bookmaking meeting, I have parents to print out kids' work in "booklet format"—each piece of paper forms four pages in the finished book. It's a bit complicated, but the pages nest inside one another and can be stitched up the center, like a real book, and then glued into the cover. If kids want illustrations, they do those at home. Some kids also include photographs with their text. We also discuss special pages that might be included: dedications, epigraphs, Tables of Contents, About the Author, Other Books by this Author, etc.

I've listed a few resources with bookmaking instructions in the *Recommended Reading* chapter, including a link to a tutorial for making books similar to the ones we've made. This sort of bookmaking is a lot of work, and you'll need as many parents as you can get to help—but it's a wonderful culminating activity, and the books are keepsakes.

Leave time for kids to share their work at the end of the meeting, and consider having a potluck feast of sorts. Make-your-own sundaes, with families providing various toppings, are always a hit in my workshops.

> *The idea of producing a book as a final product was always anticipated with excitement. –Jenny, parent of former participant and current college student*

A reading and anthology

Another option, which my older workshop kids have enjoyed, is to hold a reading with parents attending. Each child reads a favorite piece, or an excerpt from a piece, and we all, parents included, offer brief positive feedback. Parents who don't usually attend the workshop always enjoy being part of the process. We distribute an anthology of the pieces read: each kid submits a copy of his or her work; I collect them via email and have them copied and bound. You might have kids write an *About the Author* paragraph to include. Each child receives a copy of the anthology.

A friend who facilitates workshops has another way of building anthologies: each child brings enough copies of his or her contribution for every member of the group. Copies are laid out on a table and members collate their own copies, adding their own illustrated cardstock cover. Some kids may enjoy having their anthologies signed by other members, yearbook-style.

You could also consider creating an online anthology, and providing everyone with a link to the page. CheckThis (www.checkthis.com) is a simple, free platform for sharing information without creating a website or blog.

Again, you might end such a gathering with treats. It's a celebration of writers, after all!

8.
VARIATIONS ON THE WORKSHOP

You might try a variation on the regular workshop. Some possibilities:

A poetry workshop

One year I met with a group of five—which just happened to be all girls—to workshop poetry. Each week we gathered over tea and discussed a different aspect of poetry, such as word choice; simile, metaphor, and personification; sound, rhyme and rhythm; and different poetry forms. We also workshopped poetry which the girls had written and brought along. Each participant had a copy of the lovely, inexpensive anthology *Seeing the Blue Between: Advice and Inspiration for Young Poets*, by Paul B. Janeczko, which we read from both at meetings and in between them, for examples of the poetry techniques we were learning about. For our final gathering, we invited parents and had a poetry reading and tea party, complete with cucumber sandwiches and petit fours.

A teen workshop

I've done a few different variations on the workshop for teens. One year, we added a reading component. Each participant had a copy of the anthology, *Who Do You Think You Are? Stories of Friends and Enemies,* edited by Hazel Rochman and Darlene Z. McCampbell. For each meeting, I assigned a short story to be read at home, and we discussed it during our meeting, exploring the writer's craft. These discussions often dovetailed nicely with our workshopping of the kids' pieces.

Once these same teens had experienced the workshop format for a year, I structured the next year's workshop more like the adult writing classes I've taken. Participants submitted their work to each other and to me via email a week before our meetings. We read the work, and responded in writing directly on the draft, with line-by-line feedback, and overall comments at the end of the piece. At our meetings, writers read aloud a favorite paragraph from the piece, put on "the cone of silence" mentioned earlier, and then the rest of us dove into feedback. Since we'd already read, reflected on and responded to the work in writing, our feedback sessions were much more deeply considered and specific. This format also allowed kids to submit longer pieces, since we weren't reading them at our meetings. Since much of the work happened at home, we met just once each month. Also, since the kids received feedback in writing, it was easier for them to mull over that feedback, and consider applying it to revisions. Which, as I've mentioned, they did!

I got a lot out of taking people's work home and being able to have the few days before the group would happen to look over, reread, and sink into each writer's piece--something that I found invaluable for improving my writing and extremely fun to boot. When we were actually at the group, discussions were allowed to be so much deeper; no one needed to feel put on the spot to come up with a detailed, well-reasoned critique as the reader read, but instead we were able to listen and hear any other things that jumped out as great, or bits that were not quite at their best.—Ingrid, former participant and current college student

A research paper workshop for teens

This is a variation I haven't tried, but I'd like to. I'd consider working with the text *The Curious Researcher*, by Bruce Ballenger. This is a college-level text, which is often revised, so older editions are available at reasonable prices; you'd want each participant to own a copy. The text is designed to help students research a topic of interest and write a paper over the course of five weeks, working with a group for support and feedback. The five-week structure could certainly be adapted, however, and spread over more meetings—and the feedback could be offered in a workshop format. I like Ballenger's approach because it shows students how to research as well as how to write. It recognizes that curiosity and a "spirit of inquiry" are integral to both the research and writing process. Students are encouraged to explore topics that are meaningful to them, and to develop original ideas and a personal voice when writing. Good stuff.

9.
CONCLUDING THOUGHTS

I love to talk about writing. If you find yourself in a room with me, or sitting on a nearby bench at the park, and the word *writing* comes up, you'll see my head lift, and my ears orient towards the speaker. I can't help myself. Which is how I find myself in conversations like the one at the beginning of this book, with the woman who half-whispered, "My son hates writing." Yet for all of those hand-wringing conversations, I've had so many glowing ones with parents whose kids have participated in a writer's workshop. You've already heard from some of them here, as I've accessorized my own words with their glittering comments. I collect these conversations like heart-shaped rocks. The remarks from parents of current workshop participants who tell me how enthused their kids are about writing: the woman whose daughter writes into the night because she doesn't want to miss her turn to read at the workshop; the one whose son greets her in the morning with the words, "Will you write down my story today?" Then there's the feedback from parents of kids who have grown up and moved on from the workshop, parents who now reflect back on their workshop experiences with thoughts like this:

Being in the workshop was definitely a turning point for my son in developing his writing skills. From being a reluctant writer, he became a creative and excited writer who was eager to get his thoughts on paper. –Natalie, parent of former participant and current high school student

A turning point. I've seen the workshop become just that in the lives of many young writers over the years. In many cases, I think the workshop became the departure from one way of writing and towards another way; from a more traditional, schoolish approach towards the methods professional writers use. In *But How Do You Teach Writing?* Barry Lane writes, "Too many teachers and too many curricular guidelines assume that writing is a set of basic skills learned through daily practice while forgetting the real deal: writing is thought, writing is expression, writing is about having something to say."

Writer's workshops *are* the real deal. Kids figure out what they have to say. They get to experience — live and in real time! — how their words move others. They learn what they do well; they learn what they might want to work on. And they write.

It isn't called a writer's workshop for nothing. It's not a class for learning how to write. It's a workshop for *writers*. If your kids don't think of themselves as writers now—real, honest-to-goodness writers—the workshop will change that. So start up a workshop already! Gather those kids and let them share their stuff, and teach them how to be kind and helpful to one another.

You can cultivate writers.

part 2:

THE TOOLBOX

In this section I'll share a few other ideas for you to stash in your facilitator's toolbox. Think of these like the extras that appear on your favorite DVD: they aren't necessary for you to enjoy the film, but they can be fun and intriguing. I don't want to overwhelm you with information in this guide; at this point you know all you need to know to start facilitating a workshop. But when you're ready for a bit more, here are some ideas to develop your facilitating skills, your writing skills, and your techniques as the parent of a fledgling writer.

10.

A CRASH COURSE IN WHAT MAKES LITERATURE WORK

For the kids, they loved the attention they got from their peers, I believe, and they then had a vocabulary to talk about some of the things we were reading aloud. We talked about structure, word choice, pacing, etc. –Stefani, parent

No, I am not going to teach you how to distinguish between allegory, allusion and alliteration here. You don't need an English degree to facilitate a workshop—I don't have one! Instead, I'll just remind you of a few basics of effective writing, with examples collected over the years from the kids in my workshops.

Intriguing words, powerful verbs

Words are a writer's clay. They're the medium that writers mold, shape and manipulate, and like sculptors seeking the perfect hunk of marble, writers are always searching out the right words for the job.

"Remember then," William Zinsser wrote in his essential manual, *On Writing Well,* "that words are the only tools you will be given."

Writers gather words and audition them for the sentence at hand. Sometimes they search for a quirky, unexpected word like *bugaboo* or *fussbudget*; sometimes they seek something frank and muscular, like *wreck* or *claim*. Sometimes a sentence calls for a mellifluous, sweet-to-the-ear word: *luscious, sassafras, ceremonious*. Writers love words that sound like their meanings—a category that an English teacher would label *onomatopoeia*—and use them for their multi-layered punch: *Pop. Sizzle. Zigzag.* They might string together words with similar sounds, like I just did in this sentence. When the technique is used sparingly, it makes lines pleasing, and can give a particular sentence subtle impact. English teachers call these repeated beginning-of-word sounds *alliteration*.

In the world of words, verbs are some of the most powerful. They are, literally, where the action is. An apt verb can make a sentence come alive. The verb *walk*, for example, has dozens of synonyms, from *glide* to *totter*, and each conveys its own nuances.

Encourage your workshop kids to become word collectors, seeking out appealing ones in their lives and in their readings. Become a gang of word hounds. Suggest that kids collect words as they collect seedpods or bottle-caps—and perhaps gather favorites in a notebook.

When the kids in your workshop read their work, jot down words that catch your attention. During feedback time, point out particularly interesting and effective words. In our most recent workshop, I noted the following delights in the kids' work: *makeshift, mis-*

giving, gingerly, discombobulated, astonishment, hissed, peered, and whooped.

Recently my ten-year-old was curled up beneath a blanket on our oversized ottoman reading Rick Riordan's *The Lost Hero,* and he called to me in the laundry room.

"Crestfallen! That's a *good* word!"

Yes, it is!

Specific, sensory details

A teenage boy in one of my workshops set his story on a bus. His first paragraph included the following:

"The lady beside him tenderly lifted herself from her seat and walked down the row of passengers towards the exit. Jeff heard the two folding doors swing open, and felt the bus sink downwards exhaling a loud 'hisssssss.' Through the window, he could see three high school students waiting on the curb, wearing puffy ski jackets. The old woman started to descend the steps but was cut off by the impatient kids, who barged past her and proceeded to pay the driver."

I can feel myself on that bus. It's the sinking of the bus at the stop and the loud "hissssssss" that does it. I can see those teenagers in their down jackets, pushing past the old lady. These lines are full of detail, and not just visual detail. There's sound; there's the kinesthetic feeling of the body being lowered. The writer helps me recall what it is to ride a bus, and places me right in the scene, with Jeff and the old lady.

Detail does that. Especially detail that appeals to all the senses, that moves beyond the visual, as this writer does, that uses smells, sounds, tactile feelings, tastes.

In *Wild Mind: Living the Writer's Life,* Natalie Goldberg writes, "*Be Specific.* Not car, but Cadillac. Not fruit, but apple. Not bird, but wren. Not a codependent, neurotic man, but Harry, who runs to open the refrigerator for his wife, thinking she wants an apple, when she is headed for the gas stove to light her cigarette."

Be specific. Be concrete. This is writing advice that even young children can work with. They can grasp the notion that precise details draw a reader into a scene. For a writing exploration, you might have kids revisit a piece of previous work to search for details that could be made more specific. Or you could offer a list of generic terms—*bird, lunch, flower, toy*—and have kids riff on these with particular examples.

The kids in my workshops move me with such particulars constantly. The smell of kettle-corn at a baseball game; a diary with a blue and green cover and matching pen; gravel pressing into a fallen character's back; the sound of "my sister's uneven scooter wheels skittering along the ground like an engine that won't start."

These particulars are pearls. Recognize them when the kids in your workshop place them in their writing—that is, if the other workshop kids don't recognize them first!

Metaphorical language

A twelve-year-old in one of my workshops wrote an adventure story about a group of girls at a "school for thieves." In one scene a character becomes angry when told that she can't join a search for her missing sister. She snaps, "My sister's just been kidnapped and you think I'm going to sit here like a bookshelf?"

Sit here like a bookshelf. *That* retort caught my attention. The image of the girl stuck in her room, like a piece of furniture, was powerful. And it certainly established the protagonist as witty.

Metaphorical language usually comes in the form of simile and metaphor. If you want to get technical, similes directly compare one thing to something else; the bookshelf quote is an example. A word such as *like* or *as* often serves as the bridge. Here's another one, from a teen's description of a mischievous friend with a who has a particular grin when coming up with a daring idea: "His smile is like cake; it's fine, even fun, if you have it every now and then, but too much isn't good for you."

Metaphors, on the other (metaphorical!) hand, compare two items by leaping over the comparison and simply making the first item *become* the second. Metaphor means *to transport* in Greek; you could say that metaphors transport, or even transform, one thing into something else. The bridge between the two is invisible. An example from the workshop, from a narrator who has been running for ten hours: "The burning fire in my lungs which had started out quite small, now felt hot enough to burn down Antarctica, ice and all." Of course, the air in this narrator's lungs isn't actually fire—it just feels like fire. The writer could have written that his breath felt like fire, but describing it *as* fire makes the analogy even more direct, and stronger. It works because the reader knows what it's like to run until it feels that your lungs are on fire.

Don't get hung up on the technicalities, though. Instead, consider what metaphorical language does. It forces the reader to look at something in a new way. It slows us down and shakes our expectations. It makes us think.

I've found that kids are more likely to incorporate metaphorical language into their writing if they get some practice at it through writing explorations. Try giving them a list with unfinished phrases: as cold as _____; as frightening as _____; as fast as _____; as timid as_____, and ask them to come up with fresh, surprisingly similes. (*As cold as ice* is not fresh, no matter how fresh ice keeps other items!) The book *As Quick as a Cricket,* by Audrey Wood is good simile inspiration for younger kids. You might try something similar with metaphors. Give kids a list of nouns followed by the phrase *look like.* Snails look like _____; flowering trees look like _____; grandmothers look like _____. Have kids list as many images as they can, and then try forming their favorites into metaphorical lines, together. Just yesterday in a Twitter tweet, Anne Lamott described local flowering trees as having "afros of blossoms." I loved that.

Once kids have a grasp on metaphorical language, you can point out that similes and metaphors work best when they employ images and terminology suited to the setting and tone of the particular piece of writing. Comparing a mother to a robot in a story set in the pioneer West might not work so well; saying that she flits from one task to another like tumbleweed on a dusty road would likely be more effective.

Well-developed characters

In *Spilling Ink: A Young Writer's Handbook,* Ellen Potter writes, "I choose my characters the way I choose my friends. They interest me. I may even admire them in certain ways. They may not be perfect—in fact they're more interesting if they aren't—but I definitely want to know them better."

If characters are written well, readers will want to get to know them better too. That's important. If you're writing a story, the plot won't matter if your reader doesn't care about your protagonist. And if you're writing a nonfiction piece about an actual person, you'll want that person to be a vivid as possible.

What makes a character—or a real person—vivid and intriguing?

A variety of things. For one, specific, sensory details, which we've already explored, are just as important in establishing a unique, believable character, as they are to writing in general. A teen in one of my workshops wrote about her older brother, who had gone off to college and returned a different person: "He looks you in the eye when you talk to him, and he doesn't shift around and fidget when you are saying something that he really needs to hear." It's an insightful observation; the writer doesn't have to tell us that her brother has changed. We can see it.

There are many details that can make characters vivid: details about their appearance, what they think, how they move, what they value, what they own. The girl who can level a boy and put him in a headlock before he knows what's happened to him. A member of a pack of runaway kids who shows her authority by monitoring how much food everyone gets. We understand that the first girl is tough, and the second bossy, without the writers having to tell us directly.

Dialogue—which we'll explore more deeply in an upcoming section—can certainly convey a great deal about characters: what they say; what they *don't* say, how they say it. Are they chatty, or long-winded, or do they speak in single syllables? Do they refuse to be left behind, *sitting like a bookshelf?*

Many characters don't just speak with dialogue, however. When characters narrate a story—when the piece is written in first person, in other words—we can learn even more, from how those characters tell their tales, and what they choose to share. Since we're inside a character's mind, we know how he or she thinks. A vivid narrative voice can really engage a reader. Consider how this character, from another workshopper's story, introduces himself: "Unlike other kids my age, I don't like playing video games, hanging out at the local mall, watching movies at the local theater or playing sports. I like hunting monsters." Already, we can see that this character is atypical, possibly somewhat cynical, and definitely adventurous.

As Ellen Potter wrote in that introductory quote, characters are more interesting if they're imperfect. They may have little faults, like the Roman soldier in one boy's story, who repeatedly fails his regiment because all he thinks about is food. Or larger ones: the amnesiac girl from a teen's poem, who thinks she injured herself by falling from a bridge, but ultimately realizes that she'd attempted a suicidal jump. Flaws make characters more real, more relatable. We'll forgive their mistakes if there's enough to like in them.

We also want a character's behavior to be consistent with what we've come to know about him or her—but then again, it's good if sometimes a character surprises us slightly too. Flaws and surprises keep characters engaging.

Compelling plot

Most compelling stories contain a problem that begs for resolution. As the main character struggles with this problem, tension builds in the story. This is important. As Ralph Fletcher writes in *What a Writer Needs,* "Tension staples the reader's eyes to the page, and writers work hard to create it. Conflict remains the quickest way of creating instant tension."

This notion may take you right back to your high school English class, say, sophomore year. Just picture Mr. S. with his plaid shirt and shrub-like mustache, scrawling across the blackboard three, or five, or seven types of conflicts that occur in literature. (There always seems to be consensus on the first three, but lists vary beyond that—although the conflicts always seem to come in odd-numbered groupings, for inexplicable reasons.)

Starting every list is the *man versus man* conflict—or in our more enlightened times, *person versus person*. In these stories the main character comes up against another character, and some issue needs to be resolved before the story ends. You're likely to find plenty of these in your workshops, in the guise of everything from monster battle epics to emotional teen runaway dramas.

Then there's the *person versus nature* conflict, which is often a type of survival story. A kid in one of my workshops fictionalized a true story of a group of homeschooled campers getting lost on a hike, and turned it into an ongoing survival tale in which the situation grew increasingly dire (and increasingly comical) with every episode. The other kids clamored to hear more at each workshop—possibly because many of them were characters in the story.

There's *person versus self* in which a character struggles with his or her own doubts and demons. The struggles can be serious: a girl from a teen's poem, who tunes out the words of others because she can't cope with them; or silly: an elderly shrimp from a young boy's comic tale, who can never quite manage to stay balanced with his cane.

Some lists include categories such as *person versus society, person versus destiny, person versus the supernatural.* Don't be surprised if this last one shows up routinely in your workshop—over the years I've been introduced to many aliens, zombies and even a smart-mouthed extra-terrestrial named Trinity.

To put it simply, most intriguing stories—and even many works of nonfiction—are based on some sort of conflict. The main character's struggles with a problem are what keep the reader reading. It's useful for kids to understand this, and to know how to structure conflict into their writing. In his book *But How Do You Teach Writing?* Barry Lane funnels the process down to this: "Tell your students about what makes a good story. Tell them that all stories have three acts. The first act is the setup. This is where the author sets up the character's trouble. The second act is the mixup. This is where the character faces various obstacles. In Act 3, the story is resolved in some way."

Most kids can grasp this structure, and will enjoy looking for it in favorite books. Still, I've noticed that many kids love the lure of imagining *new* stories, and often move on to the next one before ever making it to Act 3. That's okay; it's the writer's prerogative! So long as the kids are enthused about writing, I wouldn't worry about it. Something will eventually come along that's compelling enough to stick with.

Effective dialogue

In every workshop I've ever facilitated, there have been a few kids who have a real knack for writing dialogue. They nail different manners of speech, and convey much about characters through what they say. The conversation in their work is lively, and it propels their stories. I imagine that these kids are particularly auditory learners, and they've naturally picked up the nuances of speech.

Consider this line from a pithy, no-nonsense scientist, written by a teen: "'I'm Cal McKee.' She saw him open his mouth and anticipated the question, rattling off the usual answers. 'Yes, it's a nickname; no, I won't tell you what it's for.'"

Or a dim teen's line—written by a teen—in a *Twilight* parody: "And I so *totally* agree that it's a good idea to use more than one *gawd* for a situation like this."

Or consider these lines from an eight-year-old girl, in her original tale based on Beverly Cleary's Ramona Quimby books:

"How was kindergarten?" her mother asked in a tired voice.

"It was fine except I gave Davy one of my worm rings and he said, 'Yuck!' and he threw it back at me."

"Oh Ramona," Mrs. Quimby said.

"Will you read me a story, Mama?"

"Oh Ramona, I've got a headache, and look at all those dishes I've got to put in the dishwasher." She groaned as she pointed towards the sink full of dishes.

"I'm going to lie down in the bedroom. You go play and stay out of mischief!"

This young writer has not only picked up on the details of parent-child conversation—complete with the mother's *Oh Ramona* sighs—but she's also internalized and replicated Cleary's dialogue style quite effectively.

All of the kids in your workshop can learn from the talented dialogue writers. Just note what these kids do well. They likely pare down their dialogue to the most interesting lines; they don't write every word that someone would say in real life. That gets dull. They probably vary manners of speech according to who's speaking. They know how to make some characters garrulous and others tentative. They know how to use lingo appropriate to particular characters.

The mechanics of writing dialogue can be a bit tricky. How often do you need to add a dialogue tag like *he said?* And when do you add that tag—at the end of a character's speech, or in the middle? Reading aloud at the workshop helps kids work out these issues. A girl in one of our workshops refused to use dialogue tags, choosing instead to simply write one character's words after another's. The listening kids became confused, and said so, which was a perfect lesson on the importance of tags. Other times listeners have pointed out when a writer has used the word *said* repeatedly, and we've discussed how you don't need a dialogue tag *every* time someone speaks, and how there are many alternatives to the word said: whispered, cried, replied, grunted, responded, sang. (Although going overboard with alternatives to *said* can sound amateur as well. In most cases *said* is perfectly effective, with its neutrality and unobtrusiveness.) Reading aloud is one of the best ways to finesse dialogue.

And dialogue is another skill in which kids can learn a good deal from each other.

Vivid setting

Setting, on the other hand, is an element that many kids tend to skip over. I imagine that in their youthful enthusiasm, they'd rather bypass descriptions of place for more titillating story elements like plot and character.

Yet if you want to draw a reader into your writing, it's vital that you establish the world surrounding your characters. In *What a Writer Needs*, Ralph Fletcher writes, "The writer who can create a believable world, a convincing place, goes a long way toward trancing the reader into the larger world of the article, biography, poem, or story."

Kids get better at developing settings as they get older. Consider this description from a young teen's science fiction tale:

"Z was glad to be in a more sheltered area—those clan members hadn't looked kind. He walked cautiously down the alleyway. Globs of deep blue liquid dripped off the walls next to him, and the floor was littered with shredded masses of garbage. He picked his way around them, careful not to touch the walls. He passed several decrepit doors, until he reached the one he wanted. It was made of a reinforced cardboard, which was rotting unpleasantly. The keyreader next to it had been smashed until it was almost unrecognizable, but somehow it still worked."

Writing explorations are a great way to develop skills of scene-writing with kids. Try this: Ask kids to consider a favorite character from something they've written. If they tend to write nonfiction, they can think of a real person from their own work, or consider a character from a favorite book. Ask the kids to place that character inside a room in which the character likes to spend time. It works best if the room belongs to the character, and is filled with (or devoid of) his or her possessions. Have kids write a description of the room. What items does it contain? Are there any items currently in use: a splayed book, a pile of paperclips being shaped into a mysterious contraption? Is the room filthy, Spartan, colorful, crammed-full? Is it a quiet space, or are there sounds? What sounds? What adorns the walls? Is the room old or new? Are there windows? With views of what?

Such explorations are fun, and will help kids see how much surroundings can define a character.

Ability to write in a particular genre's style

It's essential, if you want to write mysteries, to know a thing or two about plotting, and how to get the gears in a reader's mind clicking without revealing too much, too fast. If you want to write historical fiction, you should know something about your chosen time in history, including the vocabulary and speaking style of the time. If you want to write poetry, you should appreciate the value of Every Single Word.

Each writing genre has its own nuances and demands.

Sounds like this would be a tricky skill for kids to pick up, doesn't it? It isn't. I'd say that it's one of the easier techniques for kids to master. Kids can be quite adept at reproducing the nuances of a particular genre *so long as they are allowed to write in genres of choice.* When they write in the genres that they love to read, especially, they are likely to display a grasp of that genre that may astound you.

Check out the first lines from a ten-year-old's story, and his sense of how fantasy fiction works:

"I ran through the woods, dodging trees right and left. I heard yells as the guards closed in. I leaped over a creek, ran up a hill, leaped over a fallen log and turned around. There were about two-dozen guards chasing me. Most of them wielded crossbows, scimitars, hatchets or pikes. At the front, one of them was carrying a huge black flail. Arrows whizzed by, hitting trees where I'd been, seconds before. I felt in my bag. It was still there, thankfully. I ran through a clearing and then made my fatal mistake."

This writer has learned from reading and listening to fantasy fiction. Even at a young age, he's figured out how to craft an exhilarating paragraph and how to enthrall readers with foreshadowing.

Look at how this teenage girl understands the power of words and pacing in poetry:

"My parents were young

Freshman year of high school

I was a mistake."

As the poem progresses, we discover how deeply disturbed and reclusive this teenage character is; this potent early stanza helps us start to understand why.

Or consider the start of this epic poem, from a teen who admired Homer's *Iliad*:

"Tryphondus, son of Laerton and brother to Sanaesteus, was saddened/His spear was long, but it had not yet found its mark/For not one Trojan had fallen dead on its tip that bloody day."

This writer has clearly picked up a thing or two about the Greek epic poetry tradition through his personal reading.

You will likely find kids in your own workshop delving into specific genres, everything from poetic odes to science fiction to historical biography. They probably don't need to be taught much about how to do it—their favorite authors are their teachers. Simply point out what they're doing well: when they use cliff-hangers in their mystery stories; kernels of truth in their parodies; descriptions of nature in their haiku.

And then watch them take their chosen genre and run with it.

An aside on nonfiction

Writing fiction isn't for everyone! As I've written to the point of redundancy in this guide, workshop kids should be allowed to choose what to write about. Trouble is, many kids, especially younger ones, feel compelled to write stories. This may be because it's what people expect of younger kids; it may be because stories get particularly enthusiastic workshop feedback; it may simply be that kids haven't experienced enough effective models of nonfiction to know how to delve into the form. Help kids see the wide variety of writing possibilities: essays, reports, articles, interviews, biographies, scientific writing, reviews, lists. (You might also encourage other genres beyond nonfiction and straightforward fiction, such as poetry, songs, scripts, humor.) Congratulate kids for trying varied genres. Read snippets from inspiring professional writers in genres the kids haven't tried. Help the kids to value all forms of writing, and to find formats exciting to each individual child.

What does this have to do with the elements of literature? Well, it's easy to see how the elements we've explored here apply to fiction. But here's what you may not realize: the best nonfiction also employs fiction's toolbox. This has become truer than ever in the past fifty years or so, with the rise of new journalism, creative nonfiction and memoir. Simply check out an article in *National Geographic,* or a feature story in your weekend newspaper, or a critically-acclaimed memoir to see those literary elements in action. You'll find intriguing words and powerful verbs, of course, and compelling details. You may also discover metaphorical language. But there's more: a biographical piece will include characters as compelling as any in fiction; an interview will be full of intriguing dialogue; a scientific article may be grounded in real-life scenes set in vivid settings. Although nonfiction writers don't invent characters, dialogue and settings, they certainly shape and craft those elements in their work.

Help the kids in your workshop see beyond the formulaic essays and reports so prevalent in traditional classrooms, and into the possibilities of beautifully crafted nonfiction. These days, the children's section of most libraries is packed with fantastic models.

Bottom line: this crash course in what makes literature work shouldn't be reserved for fiction.

Further reading

If you want to delve a bit further into elements of effective writing, I recommend Ralph Fletcher's book, *Live Writing*. It's a book written for older kids, say ten and up--which means it's perfect for you too, because the writing in concise and engaging! Fletcher covers topics such as character, conflict, setting and endings. He goes into more depth than I do here, but it's still a slim paperback and a breezy read. And if you have older kids, make sure to leave the book lying on the kitchen table, enticingly. They might like it too.

Fletcher's longer book, *What a Writer Needs*, is also fantastic. It's a more in-depth exploration of literary techniques, but it's written for teachers and it may have more information than you need right now. Keep it in mind.

11.
IDEAS FOR WRITING EXPLORATIONS

This is just a sampling of explorations that kids in my workshops have enjoyed over the years. Other sources for explorations are listed in the *Recommended Reading* chapter. Once you get started, you'll likely find yourself coming up with explorations of your own.

Best Day Ever. Each child folds a paper into 8 sections. Have kids write about their ideal day--complete fantasy encouraged! Each section can be a different hour or time of day, with a sentence or more, and an illustration if desired.

Would You Rather. Read *Would You Rather*, a picture book by John Burningham. Then have the kids write or illustrate their own *would you rather...* statements. Hilarious.

My Animal Friends. Read excerpts from *Our Animal Friends at Maple Hill Farm* by Alice Provensen, a picture book with quirky, funny prose portraits of animals on the farm. Have kids write similar portraits of their own pets or other animals.

Analogy Explorations. Give kids papers with lines like: *as little as*_____, and have them fill in their own similes. Possibilities: *as happy as, as flat as, as purple as, as scared as, as prickly as, as warm as, as shiny as, as hungry as, as miserable as, as big as, as ridiculous as.* Encourage kids to think beyond the expected clichés. For younger kids, *Quick as a Cricket*, a picture book by Audrey Wood, is a good companion to this activity.

Bragging Contest. Have kids complete a phrase like *I'm so big that…* or *I'm so strong that…* or *I'm so smart that…* Urge them to extend their bragging beyond one line. Write a paragraph. Be a superhero! Boast shamelessly!

Make a List. Lists can be a less intimidating way into writing for some kids, or a good warm-up. Have kids make lists such as *Good Things/Bad Things; What I'm Into This Month; Things That Drive Me Nuts; Things That Are Not True About Me; Quirky Habits My Family Has; How to Get What You Want From Your Parents; 10 Things to Do at Target.* (That last suggestion came via one of my workshop kids—it's a fun one!)

Mystery Descriptions. Have kids write a particularly vivid description of an animal, or an object, and have other kids guess what it is. Write in first person. *I am a mammal that is smaller than a shoebox…*(The idea is to write a *vivid* description, not a confusing one that no one can guess.)

Show, Don't Tell. This is classic advice for writing students. Give kids a line, and have them describe what the line says, without actually saying it. Examples: *The bedroom was messy.* (Kids love this one!) *The man was* *old. The castle was beautiful. The pizza was tasty. The playground was fun.*

Creature Creator. Read aloud descriptions of mythical creatures from a *Harry Potter* volume, or a similar book. Choose examples with detailed descriptions. Have kids describe their own invented creatures in writing. They might enjoy drawing their creatures first.

Vivid Verb Charades. Have a kid act out a verb that you've conveyed to them secretly. For example, ask the child to *creep* across the room. The other kids call out verbs that describe how the actor is moving. While trying to guess the particular verb the kid is acting out, they'll inevitably call out many other wonderful, vivid verbs as well. Other verbs to have them act out: *slither, bounce, swagger, prance, sashay, zoom, stroll, trudge, stumble...* The idea is to help them discover that there are far more interesting ways to say that a character *went* across a room.

Play with Plot. Give kids a list of settings and have them brainstorm problems that might happen there. For example: *a playground*—maybe a big kid won't let others go down the slide; or the merry-go-round flies off its axel and into the air, with kids on it; or someone is vandalizing the playground at night; or when a boy goes down a slide, he just keeps going and going and ends up in an underground world...Other settings to brainstorm: *a farm, a pirate ship, a grocery store, a campground, a ballpark, a castle...* If they're interested, they can write their problem into a story.

Lingo Love. Define *lingo* to kids: specialized vo-cabulary of a particular field of interest. For example, I'm a knitter, and I toss around phrases that only make sense to other knitters, such as *LYS* (local yarn store), *UFO* (unfinished object), and *frog* (to rip out errors--rip it, rip it!) Have kids choose a personal field of inter-est and list lingo related to that interest. I've had kids make lingo lists of everything from Ultimate Frisbee to baking to Magic The Gathering cards. It's fun to ex-plore how well-used lingo can give texture to writing.

Haiku. Haiku are doable for most kids. The standard structure is a line of five syllables, followed by a line of seven syllables, then a line of five. (Although tradition-al Japanese haiku isn't necessarily so structured.) Haiku can be especially fun if the kids get silly with them, or write about items you might not typically think of as haiku fodder: *Sharpie pens, iPods, trolls, root beer.* You might give them a list of possible topics, but encourage them to come up with their own.

Specific Nouns. Give kids a list of generic nouns. Have them list specific examples for each, trying to paint the most visual picture possible. Example: *in-sect*—a yellow and green-striped caterpillar with fifty tiny feet. Other generic nouns for them to "paint": *a fruit, a car, a bird, a candy, a building, a dog.* It isn't enough to say that a character drove up in a car; we want to see the light blue Pinto with the fake wood paneling.

Two Truths and a Lie. Have kids write down two true facts or anecdotes about themselves, and a single fabricated one. Read aloud and see if kids can guess which are lies. Develops both imagination and writing skills!

Explore Your Thesaurus. Have kids bring thesauruses from home, if they have them, and discuss how to use them. Together, look up the same word in different thesauruses, to compare what different versions offer. (Personally, I love *The Synonym Finder* by J. I. Rodale.) Then have kids choose a piece of their own writing to work with, encouraging them to reread and substitute more powerful words, with the help of the thesaurus.

Put You In Your Place. Described in the Setting section of the chapter *A Crash Course in What Makes Literature Work.* Have kids take a character from their writing, or a favorite character from literature, and place him or her in a room that the character belongs in. How is the room decorated, and what items does it contain? Is the room neat or messy, cluttered or spare? Are there sounds in the room? What can you see from its windows? When we did this exploration during a workshop, the kids noticed how different the settings were for various characters, and we laughed at what might happen if we put different characters into each other's settings. So we tried it: each kid offered his or her setting to the child to the left, and the kids wrote about what their characters did in the new, unlikely settings. We wound up with a modern-day thief girl in a knight's treasury; a dragon in an extra-terrestrial's kitchen; and a runaway boy in the living room of a talking, chain-smoking trout.

Captions and Quotes. Cut out interesting pictures from magazines like *National Geographic.* Glue each picture on a separate piece of lined paper; have at least one paper for each kid. Start with all the papers on a table in the center. Each kid takes a paper and writes a caption or a quote to accompany it. When a kid finishes, he or she puts it back on the table and takes another. Work in silence and continue until there are several captions and quotes for each picture. The kids will inevitably get silly and try to outdo one another and hilarity will ensue. When finished, pass out papers and have kids read aloud a few favorites.

Change That Tense. Copy a paragraph written in third person from a book. Give each kid a copy; have them rewrite the paragraph in first person—or even second person (*you walk up the stairs.*) They may have to make a few alterations to keep each sentence logical. Discuss how changing tense changes the tone and feeling of the paragraph. Kids can also do this with sections of their own writing.

Freewrite. Freewriting is a great strategy for older kids who are fluent writers. Get them in the habit of writing for five to ten minutes at a time without stopping. Tell them not to worry about going off-topic, not to worry about correcting or editing themselves. A fun way to start is to have them write a noun at the top of their page, and then write from there and see where it takes them. When finished, have kids look back at what they wrote and underline any intriguing words or phrases. Freewriting can also be a good first brainstorming step when starting a new piece.

Freewrite Long, Freewrite Short. Have older kids choose a topic and write about it in one continuous sentence for ten minutes. No stopping, no punctuation. Later in the workshop, have them write about the same topic, but this time in lines of four words or less. Every sentence needs a subject and a verb. Compare the two types of writing. Both long sentences and short, choppy ones have their own power. Have kids search for particularly powerful lines of each type and underline them.

Make a Playlist. Another one for older kids. Have kids freewrite on a topic, such as *my weekend*, and then design a record album or playlist based on that freewrite. Don't tell them about the album exploration until after the freewrite! They come up with an album title based on their freewrite and then make up song titles to go with it. I've had kids write playlists of everything from rock operas to classical movements, all based on what they do on a typical weekend. The kids in my workshops have had a blast with this.

12.
BECOME A WRITER YOURSELF

If you want to help kids with writing, you really need to write yourself. I don't mean that you need to be a professional writer. I don't mean you need to spend a lot of time writing. But you need to write regularly, in some format. You need to know what it is to wrestle with words and push them around and replace them until they fall into an order that communicates what you mean to say. Until they become something pleasing to you. That's what writers do, and that's what kids who write well do. If you want to facilitate meaty conversations about writing in your workshop, you need to write.

Writing doesn't take a lot of time, and it shouldn't be a chore. It can, in fact, be a very satisfying joy. A few ideas for parents who would like to write more:

Craft your Facebook updates and Twitter tweets.

I hear your protests—but that's not *real* writing! Sure it is! It's words on a screen, and that's writing. By *crafting* your updates and tweets I mean selecting each word with care, and trying to add some style and personality to your lines. Are you funny in person? Are you introspective and reflective? Cheeky and direct? Dreamy and poetic? Smart and cynical? See if you can get more of your personality across with the words you choose, and the length and rhythm of your lines. Pay attention to friends on Facebook and tweeters on Twitter who have a style that you admire. How do they do it? Consider "favoriting" their posts, or keeping a compilation of them so you can study them. When writing your own updates and tweets, try pulling out a thesaurus so you can hunt for just the right word as you write, and expand your vocabulary. I know, I know, the idea of using a thesaurus for social networking may sound a bit ridiculous, but if Facebook or Twitter are your preferred forums for writing, you may as well work on your craft there—and a thesaurus can be a writer's best friend. (Don't use it to find orotund and rococo words like *orotund* and *rococo*, though, when *pretentious* or *flamboyant* are available and, well, less pretentious. Rather, use the thesaurus to find that word that's on the tip of your tongue, or one that adds a little rhythm and musicality to your line.)

Explore the world of blogging.

Blogging can be a fantastic way to develop your voice as a writer. It automatically gives you a forum for your words and, with luck and time, an audience that *responds* to your writing! If the thought of starting a blog sounds overwhelming, begin by searching for inspiring blogs to simply read. Google up a topic that interests you—homeschooling, beekeeping, photography, even something somewhat obscure, like kombucha-brewing—and then look at the search possibilities in the left column of the Google results page and click on "blogs." Viola! A bunch of blogs on your topic of interest. Click around and find some you like. You can subscribe to them via an RSS feed reader like Google Reader, or Live Bookmarks on Firefox. As you read those blogs and their comments, you'll find a web of other blogs that you also might enjoy. Leaving comments (well-crafted!) on blogs you admire is a great way to get started in the world of blog-writing.

Look for blogs that have not only content that you enjoy, but also excellent writing. One of my favorites has always been Orangette: orangette.blogspot.com Sure, I'm a foodie, and I appreciate what Molly Wizenberg writes about cooking and eating, but I especially enjoy her writing: her funny voice, her way with metaphor, her chatty, intimate style ("Actually, I should warn you: it may seem as though you have *too much* chopped pistachio to cram onto the top of the cake, but you must persevere.") Sometimes I even copy one of Molly's posts into a Word document and highlight the lines I admire, studying what she's doing. Dissecting the work of writers you admire is one of the best ways to learn the craft of writing, and no formaldehyde is involved.

If you decide to start blogging yourself, you can dip your toes in slowly. You can keep your posts private at first, and limit your audience. Or you can just dive into the deep end, publish them publicly and see what happens. There are free blogging platforms at WordPress (www.wordpress.com) and Blogger (www.blogger.com). If you have any inkling in this direction, do it! Read this comment from Rachel, a reader of my blog, WonderFarm: "My high school was a small private college prep school and we did a lot of writing. You know what I learned? That I hated writing. Or so I thought. Then, several years ago, I started blogging...what I found while blogging is that I LOVED writing." I hear this again and again from fellow bloggers. The takeaway: blogging makes writers. It can also help you discover what matters to you. I had no idea that I'd find a calling in helping parents with their kids' writing until I wrote a few blog posts about it, and people responded, and asked for more.

Write poetry.

Some of us feel particularly drawn to poetry–or songwriting. Poetry is a unique writing format: it's concise, powerful, lyrical, emotional, condensed, rhythmic, allegorical. If poetry intrigues you, one of my favorite inspirational resources is *poemcrazy* by Susan G. Wooldridge. (All books mentioned in this section are listed in the *Recommended Reading* chapter.) The book is beautifully written and fun to read. It's also full of simple, playful poetry ideas to try out yourself. (Many of which your kids may enjoy too, as Wooldridge has a long history as a poet in the schools.) The word ticket activity shared throughout the book is one of my all-time favorite writing explorations.

Read writing instruction manuals for inspiration.

Anne Lamott's *Bird by Bird* is always at the top of my–and practically everybody's–list. Her chapter "Shitty First Drafts" is possibly the best writing encouragement you will ever receive. Plus, along with her pep talks, you'll get to enjoy some of the most hilarious, irreverent and bittersweet writing around. Read her book and then take her advice and write about school lunches. You'll be amazed at what you'll find in your paragraphs.

Natalie Goldberg's books are also good, combining brief lessons about writing with engaging personal stories. *Writing Down the Bones* is a classic, but I like *Wild Mind* in particular because it contains "Try This" exercises, or prompts (which I'll delve into below.)

Several Short Sentences About Writing by Verlyn Klinkenborg is a newer favorite. In a unique style which reads like a prose poem, Klinkenborg helps would-be adult writers to consider what they learned about writing in school, and to contrast that with what effective writers actually do. It's a fantastic guide for shaking detrimental, schoolish thinking about writing, and developing your own authority as a writer. (And it may be helpful for parents who don't want to pass along their own school-thought about writing to their kids.)

Pen on Fire: A Busy Woman's Guide to Igniting the Fire Within by Barbara DeMarco-Barrett is great if you're a woman and you're, well, busy. It shows how you can work at your writing, even if you have only fifteen minutes a day. (Barbara's podcast *Writers on Writing* is another favorite resource: www.barbarade marcobarrett.com/writersonwriting/index.html   There you'll find hundreds of fantastic interviews with writers on the art and business of writing.)

Also if you're a mother, you may enjoy the book *Use Your Words: A Writing Guide for Mothers* by Kate Hopper. I love this one because it combines writing encouragement with excerpts from the work of some talented mother-writers. The excerpts are all on the topic of parenthood, and they're wonderful. The book has you studying these master writers to learn about craft, and then it offers writing prompts based on your reading. That right there is the formula for becoming a better writer: study the masters and write yourself. Highly recommended.

Keep a journal, or a writers' notebook.

If you haven't kept a journal since you were fifteen, maybe it's time to try again. A journal can be anything you want it to be. You can write recollections of your day. You can ramble on about piddly thoughts that you'd never want to admit to anyone. You can keep lists, you can experiment with style, you can play with writing prompts, described below.

You can keep a parent's journal, in which you record the memorable things your kids say and do—because no matter how memorable they are, if you don't write them down, they're bound to be forgotten.

You can record your kids' interests and wacky accomplishments, and your insights about it all. I've kept a few since my oldest was born. I don't write in mine very often anymore, but even once every few months captures a nice snapshot in time. You may plan, as I do, to share yours with your kids one day.

You can also try keeping a writer's notebook, full of ideas to use in other writing. You might collect conversations you overhear, or scenes you happen upon. You could gather quotes from other writers, or seeds for a new story or poem. I like using sticky page tabs to section off my notebook. Ralph Fletcher has a neat little paperback written for older kids called *A Writer's Notebook*, which has good ideas for organizing such a notebook, whether or not you're a kid. Or you could simply collect the same wonderful bits on index cards, as Anne Lamott writes about in *Bird by Bird*. Lamott likes index cards because they fit in her pocket, and don't make her "look bulky." She writes, "So whenever I am leaving the house without my purse...I fold an index card lengthwise in half, stick it in my back pocket with a pen, and head out, knowing that if I have an idea, or see something lovely or strange or for any reason worth remembering, I will be able to jot down a couple of words to remind me of it."

Good advice.

Respond to writing prompts.

A prompt is simply a suggestion aimed at generating juicy writing. It might be: *Write a letter to yourself at sixteen.* Or *If you could place yourself in any film, which would you choose, and why?* Even as a kid, I disliked required prompts in school, but prompts as *possibilities* are different. Browse a few, and choose one that tickles you. Prompts can help you expand your repertoire, and explore ideas you might never happen upon on your own.

Most of the books mentioned in this chapter have prompts. This Tumblr site by Luke Neff—who seems like a pretty wonderful writing teacher—has hundreds of thought-provoking ones: writingprompts .tumblr.com/ Many are aimed at students, but there are plenty to inspire an adult. Online parenting magazine *Literary Mama* posts prompts based on its contents several times a month on its blog: literarymama.com/blog/ *Rip the Page* by Karen Benke is a book of fun writing prompts for kids—which you might enjoy as well. You could even try out some of them alongside your kids.

Read and study the art of writing.

If you're an avid reader, you might enjoy studying the craft in what you're reading. Studying the masters is an essential part of becoming a writer. *Reading Like A Writer* by Francine Prose shows you how to slow down with close reading to examine how master writers do what they do. It's a fascinating book. Along similar lines is *The Well-Educated Mind* by Susan Wise Bauer, which is a guide to reading classic literature. While I prefer the content of *Reading Like a Writer,*

The Well-Educated Mind offers specific instructions for making a written record of your book study, which might make it worth consulting if that appeals to you. (And you know what I'm going to tell you: written reflection is good writing practice!) The ideas there could certainly be applied to other books, beyond the classics.

13.
A FEW THOUGHTS ON TAKING DICTATION FROM KIDS

It was really great for me to watch my son discover his voice as a writer. The voice he discovered through the freedom of narrating to a scribe (me), carried through into his independent writing. While he still prefers to narrate, when he is required to write (think standardized testing) he can confidently fill a page and a half. –Carrie, parent

Taking dictation from kids can be a powerful way to develop their voices as writers. By dictation, I simply mean writing down something that a child wants to have written down. It could be a story, but it could just as easily be a theory about life on Mars, or a description of a fairy house just built, or the words of a ditty that you catch your child singing as he eats his toast.

Powerful as it is, dictation is rarely used in schools because the adult-child ratio doesn't allow it. Yet it has great potential for homeschooling families, and for parents who work with their schooled kids at home. It can be useful for kids of all ages: from those just beginning to talk to older teenagers who might be struggling to express something in writing. I always encourage the parents of my workshop kids to consider recording the kids' workshop contributions via dictation, if that would be helpful—and even older kids can find it helpful. Dictation allows kids to focus on the content of what they'll be sharing at the workshop, rather than getting slowed down by the physical writing or keyboarding.

Dictation is helpful because learning to write is hard. I believe it's one of the hardest childhood tasks that kids take on. On my website, there's an exercise called Take Five Minutes and Try This (patriciazaballos.com/2009/10/23/take-five-minutes-and-try-this/) It will help you understand how ridiculously challenging it is to be a fledgling writer—and it really does take just five minutes.

The exercise will help you see the difference between being a fledgling writer and a fluent one. Fluency is what educators call the ability to write without thinking much about what our hands are doing, or how letters should be formed, or how to spell each word. For the most part, a fluent writer can concentrate on his or her thoughts, rather than the task of transcribing those thoughts to the page.

Young, developing writers don't yet have this fluency. Instead, they must focus on a single letter, and then the letter that comes next. While more fluent kids are able to hold an entire sentence in their minds and work toward the end of it, less fluent kids lose track of where they are as they struggle to remember if the belly of a D faces right or left, or to wonder why *when* looks funny when they spell it *oen*. (If that spelling–a favorite of my oldest at six–looks odd to you too, say the word aloud to understand where it comes from.)

Developing fluency takes years. Just as it takes years for a child to learn to speak in full sentences, in a mostly conventional way, to go from saying *ba ba ba* to *why can't I have my dessert first?* Writing is even more complicated. There's the formation of those letters to consider, and how to combine those letters to form words, and how to string those words together into sentences that make sense. Most likely it will take three, or four, or five years—or more—before a child can write without much thought to those details, and can focus on the ideas he or she hopes to transcribe to the page.

With talking, we allow children that babbling *ba ba ba* time. We let their speech develop naturally—some kids say their first words at ten months, others at eighteen. They move from single words to simple sentences when they're ready. But with writing, our society seems pressed on forcing the process along. As soon as kids hit the first grade, we push the responsibility of writing at them like it's a basket of dirty laundry and a box of detergent, expecting them to take over the task, saying in effect, it's your job now, kid.

I'd like to suggest a different model.

Instead of expecting our kids to write at six, we can let their writing develop more slowly, more organically, like we did when they learned to talk. It's likely that their writing might first consist of a word or two labeling a drawing, or a sign made for a lemonade stand, or a name attached to a gift.

Meanwhile, as their writing develops naturally, we take dictation from them. Some benefits:

- Dictation allows kids to express themselves freely, without being limited by their mechanical writing skills.
- Dictation lets them convey higher-level ideas, which they may not be capable of writing on their own.
- Dictation encourages longer, more complicated sentences and words, which are likely to get lost when a fledgling writer transcribes on his or her own.
- Dictated writing allows a child to share his or her written expression with others. It helps kids begin to see the value of capturing one's words on a page.
- The process of seeing their words transcribed allows kids to painlessly pick up on writing mechanics: spelling, grammar, punctuation. Learning these skills in the context of their own writing makes those skills pertinent, valuable and interesting to a child. (Rather than boring as a book of math drills.)
- Conversations about content that occur while kids dictate help them begin to think like writers.
- Young children tend to be expressive, creative speakers. They haven't developed self-consciousness when they speak. Dictation allows them to capture that voice, and apply it to their written expression. On the other hand, when kids

must write on their own, taking years to develop written fluency, the naturally expressive voice of childhood has often disappeared by the time they've developed the skill to transcribe it.

- Time spent taking dictation is time in which a parent is immersed in the ideas of the child. It can be a joyful parent-child experience.

- Dictation allows a child to develop a *voice* as a writer. This, I will argue, is the most important writing skill we can pass along to our children. The mechanics of writing get mastered over time–they do–but some kids never develop a written voice, a confidence and personal style on the page. Dictation helps them develop those skills from the start.

For further reading on the topic of dictation, please see the month-long series on my website titled The Dictation Project (http://patriciazaballos.com/the-dictation-project/)

14.
RECOMMENDED READING

books on teaching writing:

Live Writing; How Writers Work; and *A Writers Notebook*, all by Ralph Fletcher. I highly recommend these books, written for older kids, for *you*. *Live Writing* especially, as it discusses the basics of effective writing simply, in a very readable, well-written format. It covers character, voice, setting, conflict and more. *How Writers Work* discusses issues writers face, such as getting started, brainstorming, revision and writer's block. *A Writer's Notebook* helps the reader develop his or her own notebook for collecting writing ideas. It can be fun to help kids start notebooks during your workshop. All three books are short, easy to read and inexpensive.

What a Writer Needs by Ralph Fletcher. Covers much of the same material as in the first two books mentioned above, but written for adults. Goes into more depth, and gives examples from kids' writing.

If You're Trying to Teach Kids How to Write...You've Gotta Have This Book! by Marjorie Frank. Written for teachers of writing, but the smorgasbord style of the book makes it easier to read than some of the more academic books for teachers. Explains the workshop approach to writing, and describes the tools and techniques that writers use. Includes activities that can be adapted into workshop writing explorations.

But How Do You Teach Writing? A Simple Guide for All Teachers by Barry Lane. Although this book is written for teachers, it does an excellent job of examining the traditional school approach to writing (which most of us experienced as kids) and showing why it doesn't work. A good resource for gaining a sense of what kids really need to learn to write well. Written in a humorous, accessible style.

Spilling Ink: A Young Writer's Handbook by Anne Mazer and Ellen Potter. Another book for kids, which can also be useful to adult facilitators. Written by two children's book authors, it covers both craft and typical challenges writers face, in an engaging way. Also shares "I Dare You" writing ideas, which can be used as writing explorations.

books with ideas for writing explorations:

Rip the Page: Adventures in Creative Writing by Karen Benke. Written for kids, this playful book is full of writing exercises and experiments, as well as encouragement from professional writers. Most of the writing ideas are quick, and ideal as workshop explorations. Highly recommended.

Games for Writing by Peggy Kaye. Writing activities for younger writers, many of which can be adapted as workshop explorations.

Wishes, Lies and Dreams: Teaching Children to Write Poetry by Kenneth Koch. Emphasis is on poetry, but ideas here apply to good writing in general. Many activities can be adapted into quick explorations.

51 Wacky We-Search Reports by Barry Lane. Another one written directly for kids. Focuses on fun ways of exploring nonfiction topics, such as writing a journal from the perspective of a cheetah, or creating recipes about historical events. Explains how to add humor to the writing. Some activities may be too elaborate for workshop explorations, but it's a great resource to own nevertheless, as it expands the possibilities for nonfiction writing, which is so often taught in a dry, dull way.

Don't Forget to Write: 54 Enthralling and Effective Writing Lessons for Students 6-18 edited by Jenny Traig. Fun writing activities by writers who have taught at 826 Valencia, a program that provides free writing classes to kids. The lessons are unique, inventive and fun, and are grouped for different age levels. Many can easily be adapted to a workshop exploration.

bookmaking resources:

When we've made books in my workshops, we've used a technique very similar to the one shown in a tutorial by Pam Petty, viewable at pampetty.com/ bookmaking.htm Rather than using wallpaper, kids bring construction paper or other fancy papers, cut to size, to use for the cover and endpapers. Paper for end-papers needs to be relatively strong; lighter, tissue-like papers aren't advised for endpapers, but can work over the mat board covers. We've had luck with a product called Yes! paste, rather than the white glue used in the tutorial. This is best applied with small squares of mat board; you'll need plenty as they need replacing often. You will also need lots of newspaper to cover your work surface, as the paste is messy and will get on the books if you don't refresh the newspaper often. Best advice: make a practice book or two before making them with the kids! And make sure you have several other parents along to help.

A few other good bookmaking resources:

Making Handmade Books: 100+ Structures, Bindings and Forms by Alisa Golden.

How to Make Books: Fold, Cut & Stitch Your Way to a One-of-a-Kind Book by Esther K. Smith.

Bookmaking with Kids website:
www.bookmakingwithkids.com

books for specialized workshops:

Titles referred to in the chapter *Variations on the Workshop.*

Seeing the Blue Between: Advice and Inspiration for Young Poets by Paul B. Janeczko, for a poetry workshop.

Who Do You Think You Are? Stories of Friends and Enemies edited by Hazel Rochman and Darlene Z. McCampbell, for a reading/writing workshop for teens.

The Curious Researcher by Bruce Ballenger, for a research paper workshop for teens.

writing books for adults:

Titles referenced in the chapter *Become A Writer Yourself*. Some contain short exercises that can support your own writing; some can be adapted for kids in a workshop.

The Well-Educated Mind by Susan Wise Bauer.

Pen on Fire: A Busy Woman's Guide to Igniting the Fire Within by Barbara DeMarco-Barrett.

Writing Down the Bones: Freeing the Writer Within and *Wild Mind: Living the Writer's Life* by Natalie Goldberg.

Use Your Words: A Writing Guide for Mothers by Kate Hopper.

Several Short Sentences About Writing by Verlyn Klinkenborg.

Bird by Bird: Some Instructions on Writing and Life by Anne Lamott.

Reading Like A Writer by Francine Prose.

Poemcrazy: Freeing Your Life with Words by Susan Goldsmith Wooldridge.

classic books on facilitating workshops, written for teachers:

These are comprehensive books, written for classroom workshops. I don't necessarily recommend them for you, as workshops of this style are likely more complicated than what you'll want to facilitate. But you might want to peruse these titles if you can find them through your library. You can browse the table of contents for most online.

Writing Workshop, The Essential Guide and *Craft Lessons* by Ralph Fletcher and JoAnn Portalupi.

The Art Of Teaching Writing by Lucy McCormick Calkins.

Writing: Teachers and Children At Work by Donald H. Graves

In the Middle by Nancie Atwell. For teachers of middle schoolers.

other books referenced in this guide:

Writing with Power by Peter Elbow

Boy Writers by Ralph Fletcher

Holding on to Good Ideas in a Time of Bad Ones: Six Literacy Principles Worth Fighting For by Thomas Newkirk

On Writing Well by William Zinsser.

ACKNOWLEDGEMENTS

Many thanks to all of the kids who have work-shopped with me over the years, who taught me how much a workshop can encourage a young writer. Special thanks to the following young people, whose writing appears in these pages: Ellie Angstadt-Leto, Sarafina Angstadt-Leto, Claire Fahrner, Luke Karl, Mariah Nuerge, Otto Olnes, Adam Rees, Henry Zaballos, Lily Zaballos and Theo Zaballos. Thanks to the parents for getting the kids to the workshop all these years, and for writing such shimmering testimonials of what a workshop can do.

Thank you to my beloved, longtime readers Melissa Mack and Carolyn Ortenburger for your ever-insightful feedback on this manuscript. Thank you to Carrie Pomeroy and Amy Bowers for reading and responding from a parent's perspective, and offering such thoughtful suggestions. Thank you to Susan Ryan for sharing your own workshop experiences here. Thanks to Pam Petty for allowing me to link to your bookmaking tutorial. And to Charlotte Cook for showing me how to dig for treasures in the written work of others.

Thanks to my sweetheart, Chris, for cooking and vacuuming and kid-wrangling as I finished up this book. Although you cook and vacuum and kid-wrangle anyway, always.

And thank you to my kiddos, Henry, Lily and Theo, for showing me how much a writer's workshop has meant in your growth as writers. I did it for you, my loves. I hope this guide will bring workshops into the lives of other kids, and that they will come to love writing as much as we have.

ABOUT THE AUTHOR

photo by Mary McHenry

Patricia Zaballos is a writer and longtime home-schooling parent of three. She has facilitated writer's workshops for kids for over a dozen years. Once upon a time she was an elementary school teacher, but her kids slowly beat the schoolteacher out of her, and helped her come to value passion-driven, project-based learning. Patricia is an avid knitter, beekeeper and chef of all things faceless. You can read more of her thoughts about kids' writing and kid-driven learning on her blog, *WonderFarm*. http//:patriciazaballos.com/blog.

Website:
patriciazaballos.com

Blog:
patriciazaballos.com/blog

Twitter:
twitter.com/Wonderfarm

Facebook:
facebook.com/patriciazaballos.wonderfarm

Look for Patricia's upcoming book,
This Is What I Want To Say:
Using Dictation to Encourage Young Writers